ONE DAY
AT A TIME
True Love Endures all

Bonnie Shetters Wise

outskirts
press

Outskirts Press, Inc.
http://www.outskirtspress.com

ISBN: 978-1-9772-3600-5

PRINTED IN THE UNITED STATES OF AMERICA

Dedication

Written with much love, in honor of:

Isaac M. Wise, Jr. (Jackie)
August 19, 1939–May 1, 2012

I pray these words will be a blessing and encouragement, whether facing a trial or difficulty in life or reading to grow in God's word. Whatever the reason, remember, God is in control, and he will provide our needs and our heart's desires if we are faithful and trusting in His word!

INTRODUCTION

One Day At A Time is the story of our love, our marriage from June 7, 1963, to May 1, 2012, our sickness, and our walk for the last nine months of Jackie's life. Our story has taught me many things that I would like to share with others who may face the same trials and victories we have encountered. I pray these words will help as you go through the trials and valleys God allows in your life.

I learned that we all have disappointments and pain in our lives, and we should remember that no one is exempt from these things. Our first thoughts are usually, "Why are these things happening to me?"

Let me assure you, God has a plan for our life and has designed every step, especially for you. Everything happens for a reason, and by His design, and one day, you will look back and say, "I understand now why that happened."

Psalm 37:4 4Delight thyself also in the Lord: and he shall give thee the desires of thine heart.

This verse tells us that God knows the desires of our hearts. When we love and serve Him, He opens our eyes, allowing us to see that love as He fulfills our hearts' desires.

PART I:

One Day At A Time

We endeavored to live One Day At A Time and trust God, knowing He would lead and guide us in the way we should go. We were not perfect, nor do we always do what was right. However, we learned many things on this walk together, and the things we learned are what I would like to share.

The following Scripture is one that went through my mind often during the last nine months of Jackie's Life:

Take therefore no thought for the morrow: for the morrow shall take thought for the things of itself. Matt. 6:34 KJV

What does this mean? How can it help me in my walk? To me, it means to live only today and not to worry about tomorrow. On June 30, 2011, it became a reality that we could just handle One Day At A Time. We could not look ahead or question, "What if?".

It is not a journey we started down one day, but gradually, slowly, and finally, it became a continual growing and learning process. I am not where I want to be because I am human, and it is human nature to worry. I believe God has done a work in my life, and I continue learning to live One Day At A Time.

1

THE BEGINNING

OUR STORY IN learning to live **One Day At A Time** together began when we married on June 7, 1963. Like many others, our love story is unique and very different from the typical we met; our eyes locked, and we were instantly in love, knowing destiny had brought us together forever. Our families had been friends since before my birth, so there was no earth-shattering first meeting.

They had moved down from Tennessee to Georgia around the same time in 1944. The Wise family moved to Yulee, Florida, and my family, Shetters, settled in Kingsland, Georgia.

Mom and Dad, Richard (RT), and Ethel (Judy) Shetters had eight children when they moved to Georgia: Mary, Richard, Johnnie, Vivian (Bib), Joe, Dean, James, and Hutch. Later, three more were added, Bonnie, Joy (Tiny), followed by the baby, Gene.

Our families, Wise and Shetters, remained close friends and spent time together in the early years after moving to Florida. We called Jackie's parents Aunt Cynthia and Uncle Ike. Years passed, and as my brothers and sisters married and move away, they now visited home on their weekends. The visits from Aunt Cynthia and Uncle Ike were not as often, and our visits to them also became less frequent.

In January 1961, my parents received a call that Uncle Ike had died in an automobile accident. Jackie was throwing up from the pain in his left side, and his family suspected he had appendicitis. They were taking him to the hospital on a rainy night when the car entered a curve. The wet road caused the car to go into a slide and leave the road. Uncle Ike died from the impact as the vehicle crashed into a tree. Rosie, Jackie's sister, received cuts and bruises, but the impact threw Jackie out of the car and into a ditch.

Jackie spent a few days in the hospital with broken ribs, a broken collarbone, cuts, and bruises. He came home from the hospital by ambulance because of the continuing pain with the slightest movement. The ambulance came back on the day of the funeral to take him, but he was unable to go.

All of our family went to their house before the funeral to spend some time with the family. I knew that Jackie blamed himself for the accident, and as we left their home driving to the church for the funeral, I thought about him and how bad he looked.

My heart was breaking as I told Mom and Dad, with all the wisdom of a fifteen-year-old, "I should have stayed there with him. He looks so bad, and he doesn't need to be there by himself."

"He will be fine," Mom assured me. "One of his friends is coming over to stay with him.

A few months after the funeral, Jackie and Rosie came to our house, and although he mainly talked with my Dad, I noticed him looking my way. Even with all the family there talking and laughing, I was sure he came to see me, and I felt that connection. I was not even allowed to date yet!

The 60s were a stressful time in our world. Vietnam was the daily news, and our young men were drafted and leaving. Some of Jackie's close friends were already in Vietnam. He believed it was his duty to serve our country, so he volunteered for the draft. I did not hear from him for almost a year after he left for boot camp.

Meanwhile, I am now in high school and dating someone I had met in class. I had noticed him before because he stood a lot taller than most of the other students - my high school sweetheart and first crush, Floyd. We dated and broke up, the typical high school teenagers—stayed mad for a few days and then dated again on the weekend unless he had a date with someone else.

Floyd and I had been bowling one Saturday afternoon, and as he parked in front of our house, he turned to me with a look of aggravation on his face. "Who is that talking to your dad?"

I had not even noticed anyone on the porch. My attention and all of my concentration were on Floyd, wondering when or if he would call me again or if he was still going out with his other girlfriends.

When I heard his words, I turned my head and looked toward my house. Whew, my heart dropped to my feet as I realized it was Jackie sitting there talking to my Dad. I finally answered: "He is just a friend of our family." Well, that was the truth!

My heart started beating like crazy. Calm down, Bonnie; this is Jackie. He has known you since you were a bratty little kid. He looked a lot different from the tall, skinny, good-looking guy I had last seen. In Uncle Sam's hands, he had developed some muscles that his Army uniform displayed very well. What a difference boot camp had made!

This visit started our story and our future. We traveled a long road together, and it left us looking back to circumstances. We saw how God uses people and everyday problems to mold and shape us into what He wants us to be. Our journey taught us what genuine love, dedication, and devotion are. I hope our story will be an inspiration and encouragement to you as you read it.

2

HIGH SCHOOL AND MY FIRST JOB

HERE WE NEED to go back in our story and return to my Andrew Jackson High School days when Floyd and I dated! I had missed school the day before, and now, standing by my locker, I was looking for him. He usually passed by on his way to class. I shifted books around, looking for the one I needed. My hands were full as I searched for it, and just as I was thinking about Floyd, he suddenly appeared, peering around my locker door.

He smiled at me, "Hey, feeling better today?" When I heard his voice and looked up at him, he leaned over and kissed me on the cheek.

Remember, this is the 60s, and things were different, and you did not go around kissing in school. We had some pretty strict rules back then, which we followed most of the time!

I was one of those rules-following people. Wouldn't you know that, of all people, this happened to me? Someone who never got into trouble would have to be the recipient of a kiss on this day when an eagle-eyed teacher happened to be on monitor duty. Her little beady eyes did not miss him as he leaned over and kissed me on the cheek. She walked over to my locker and took one book out of my hand as she said, "You can pick this up in the Dean's office after school."

"But, but it isn't"... I tried to talk to the teacher, but she raised her hand to silence me and said, "Pick it up in the Dean's office." I continued, "But.. wait."

"That is not my book," I mumbled as she walked away. I had tried to tell her, but she would not listen. So, I arrived on time at Miss Wilson's office after school to get my locker mate's book. (By the way, why did I get sent to the Dean's office, but not Floyd?)

I had never gotten into trouble at school, so embarrassment had my face a little red. I knew it would not be fun once I got there. Miss Wilson had a reputation for being strict. Shaking in my shoes is an accurate description of my actions that day!

She looked up at me as I walked in. "Have a seat, young lady, and tell me why you are here today and why do I have your book?"

Biting my lip, I nervously licked my lips and then told her, "The book that the teacher took is not mine. It is Shirley's. We share a locker, and I did not want her to get into trouble, so I came to explain and to get her book back."

"Did I also hear something about a kiss?" She asked.

I just knew I was going to die, my knees continued shaking, and I knew if she didn't kill me, my Dad would.

"I didn't know he was going to kiss me. I missed a couple of days because I was sick, and he just leaned over and kissed me on the cheek. It wasn't me; it was Floyd."

She smiled, and we talked for a while about school, then she thanked me for coming in as she handed me the book that belonged to Shirley.

Leaving as quickly as possible was my goal, but she stopped me by asking, "Bonnie, what are your plans for the future? What are you doing after graduation?"

I had no answer to that. There were no plans for the future, and college did not appear anywhere in my thoughts. (I do now have a bachelor's degree.) I belonged to the local YMCA, and my friend Glaconia and I were on a gymnastic team. I was a Jr. Leader at the Y, but there was nothing there as far as my future.

The conversation was all about me that day, my family, school, the Y, and the future. She asked me to stop by again when I had time.

After I met her, she was not anywhere near the fire-breathing dragon I thought she would be. I stopped by occasionally just to say hello and get advice once in a while. I think she saw the young girl who struggled a little with self-consciousness because of how I dressed and the things I lacked. I believe she also learned one more important thing: I had a big loving family with an even bigger heart!

Miss Wilson continued to "talk" to me when we had the opportunity. One day, she asked, "Have you ever thought about getting an afternoon job or maybe on the weekends?"

"Well, no, not really. I would not even know where to look."

"I have a friend who manages a theater. She needs someone to help with the ticket booth and the concession area if you would be interested."

My thoughts only included school, making it to graduation, and of course, Floyd.

"I will talk to Mom and Dad and let you know."

They did not approve at first, but finally, they agreed that I could work if I kept my grades up. So, I began my first job at a theater in downtown Jacksonville.

I was thankful for the job, which allowed me to buy things I would not otherwise have. Miss Wilson did more for me than she ever realized when she helped me with a job, and I will be forever grateful. I understand now that God allowed me to meet her, my mentor, and my friend. She also paid for my cap and gown rental and bought my annual my senior year.

Working at the theater taught me the work ethics I have used for the rest of my life. There is always something to do, and if you do not do it right the first time, go back and do it again. I cleaned and re-cleaned the hot dog machine. The soda fountains remained spotless, and the countertop and shelves had no fingerprints!

3

GRADUATION

FINALLY, IT IS graduation day, and I was the first and only one of eleven children to graduate. My parents were proud, although they did not say it; this was just their way. Some of my brothers and sisters would be at the Coliseum for our graduation, the Andrew Jackson class of 1963!

My brother Hutch was not there that night, but he had bought my class ring for me. God always supplied, in His time and in His way. So yes, high school was a fantastic time of learning in my life. I was excited about graduating. Jackie had started writing me letters again after Floyd and I broke up several months earlier. He was already in the Army, so we only dated a brief time. We wrote letters daily and here is where we fell in love.

In his last letter, he told me he loved me and wanted to marry me. He was shy and writing it on paper is probably the only way he could have proposed. Well, it was not exactly a proposal, but a sentence that said, "Maybe we can get married when I come home."

Really, I thought! Ever watch any romantic movies?

I learned it was his way. Straightforward, simple, but the most loving guy you would ever meet. Jackie, always quiet, doing simple little things throughout life to show how much he loved me. He was not the roses, candy, and presents kind of guy but the hand holding, arm around your shoulders, kiss me, hello and goodbye, and told me every day how much he loved me. He did not really have to say, "I love you." If you happened to be around us, you knew he did.

He always thought he was the lucky one to have me, but it was the other way around. I was so blessed to have him in my life. All of this will be in the future. Today, it is graduation day, and we will graduate in the Jacksonville Coliseum.

I did not know if Jackie had gotten home since I had not heard from him. I nervously stood in line, waiting to hear my name called, and it seemed as if it took forever to get to the S's. Finally, they called my name, Bonnie Sue Shetters, and I nervously walked across the stage, looking out over everyone there. Picking one person out in that crowd was an impossibility, and now graduation was over. Jackie is nowhere in sight.

I walked outside on the steps, hoping to find him. In his last letter, he said he would be here. There were too many people; even if he had made it, I would never find him in this crowd.

I turned around to go back in and try to locate my family. As I was walking back up the steps, I heard his voice; the one etched into my memory that I will never forget, "Looking for somebody?"

I turned in that direction, and as he smiled at me, he held his arms out. I jumped about three steps, and he caught me with a hug that only he could give. There was just something about the way he hugged you. I knew he cared for me, and I felt safe in his arms for the rest of his life. I knew when he wrapped his arms around me throughout our life together; everything would be ok, no matter what the situation.

After graduation, we stopped by my house to visit with all my family; then we rode to Yulee to spend some time with his Mom and sister. We only had a short time together, but as we rode to Yulee, he asked me to marry him. He had a one-week leave and would be home until next Friday, and of course, I said yes.

He told me he would be there the following day, and we would go to Georgia and get married. I look back on our lack of planning, and it seems crazy now. I am thankful God had a plan for us, even when we didn't have one for ourselves!

4

THE WEDDING

JACKIE CAME BACK early the next day, looking mighty handsome in his Army uniform. I had on my white graduation dress, and we held hands as we walked into the kitchen.

"Mom, we are going to get married."

Her response was, "OK." I don't think she believed me. I was the funny, crazy one in the family who was always cutting up.

We drove to Kingsland, and if I had thought about having the blood work done, I probably would have backed out. I am and have always been a needle sissy.

After the bloodwork and license, we went to Nahunta, Ga., and a preacher married us in his home. In a simple, short, and sweet ceremony, we said our wedding vow and sealed it with a nervous kiss! The preacher, seeing this nervous soldier and even more nervous, crazy young girl, asked me, "Young lady, do your parents know where you are?"

"Yes, they do," I replied with a smile. Well, Mom did, but Dad would be surprised! He had driven to Tennessee to take my grandmother home.

No ring, no music, just us, and we were happy. We did not think about where we would live, how we would live, or what we would do, but we were young and in love. (I am sure this is not what Matt 6:34 meant.)

"Take therefore no thought for the morrow: for the morrow shall take thought for the things of itself - Matt 6:34."

We drove back home, told Mom and all the family we had gotten married, and then on to our honeymoon. Remember, no money! We arrived back in Yulee and spent our few days together at home with his Mom and sister. We had no money or plans, but we had all that matter, and that was each other.

His leave was up all too soon, and he had to catch a bus to Texas. I cried as soon as the bus pulled out of sight.

Five and a half months seemed like an eternity when he returned to Ft. Hood, Texas. We communicated by writing letters every day, and only occasionally did we have the luxury of a phone call. That just made us miss each other even more. Time passed by so slowly; it seemed like years, but finally, he was coming home.

He arrived in Jacksonville, and after spending a few hours with my family, we drove to his Mom's house in Yulee. We had walked outside holding hands, walking around to be alone, planning our future, discussing our hopes and dreams. We were happy to be together again.

I will never forget that day because it was a highly anticipated day for us, and we had been counting down the days. However, it would turn into a day of sorrow for the United States of America, November 22, 1963.

Aunt Cynthia called to us and asked us to go inside. She and Rosie looked shocked and in tears. The news had broken in on the broadcast to announce to America that our President, John F. Kennedy, had been assassinated.

I don't know if anyone had ever interrupted the news or broken into any broadcast before, but it was everywhere on this day. Most people still depended on newspapers in the morning and afternoon editions. Not everyone had the luxury of having a TV, all of which were black and white.

The assassination changed our country, but it also changed TV network news forever. During that time, all Americans gathered around their TVs to watch the news, stunned by our President's assassination. I remember how Walter Cronkite's voice broke while talking about President Kennedy's death.

We have come a long way since 1963, but it is always good to remember how God has blessed us in America. I pray we never forget our lives can change in just a second, as fast as a speeding bullet.

5

TOGETHER AT LAST

WE BEGAN OUR married life in Yulee in 1963. I was not only adjusting to marriage, but I thought he had moved me to the end of the world. I moved from downtown Jacksonville on Duval Street to a dirt road and no neighbors. We had a caution light at A1A and US17, some gas stations, a grocery store, a barbershop, a liquor store, and a two-lane road to Fernandina or Callahan and Jacksonville or Kingsland, Georgia.

We became the typical young couple; I stayed home and tried to look and act like June Cleaver. I cooked him breakfast before he left for work and dinner when he came home. My cooking was not the greatest, but he would eat it and never complain.

Jackie returned to work at Rayonier Timber Division, where he worked before going into the Army. Located just across the road from our house, it gave him a quick commute to work. His job started early, so that meant he got home early in the afternoon. Warm weather found us fishing in the afternoon or riding to the beach. It is incredible to look back and realize what good times we had when life was so simple and different from today's rush and hurry world. Our friends came over. We enjoyed our picnics, fishing, or riding to the beach. Sometimes, we all get together at the drive-in movies, shared our snacks, and just relaxed and had fun.

We had been married for seven months when I started getting sick every morning. "I am going to the doctor today," I mumbled as I ran out to throw up again.

I remember the day just like yesterday. Jackie wanted to take the day off and go with me, but I told him I would be ok to drive myself. He hugged me, smiled, and said, "I love you." I sat on the porch in the fresh air while he cooked his breakfast and packed his lunch. He came outside, kissed me, and left for work with a big smile on his face.

He had a little more pep in his step as he came home that afternoon. As he set his lunchbox down, he looked at me, waiting for the answer to the question I recognized on his face. All I had to do was smile, and he came across the room in about two or three steps, wrapped his arms around me. "We are going to have a baby." Excited does not even begin to express how he was. I wish I had captured the moment on film so Isaac could have known how happy he made us, even before his birth.

Our happiness continued as we started getting accustomed to the news that we were having a baby. However, the ringing of the phone interrupted our evening with some bad news. My brother, Hutch, had been severely injured in an automobile accident. They did not know if he would survive through the night.

Our family all met at Mom and Dad's house in Jacksonville. We carpooled together, making a trip to Corpus Christi, Texas.

I threw up from Jacksonville to Texas at every gas stop and sometimes in between. Thankfully, my brother-in-law had learned to stop the car quickly when I told him I had to throw up again.

Finally, we made it to the hospital, and I rushed to his room as soon as we had his room number. I glanced at the person in bed, turned around, and came out as quickly as I had gone in.

"I don't know who that guy is, but it isn't Hutch. He is in terrible shape."

One of my sisters walked back to the nurse's station but quickly returned and said, "That is his room, and it is Hutch!"

His broken leg was up in a sling because it required another surgery. They did not know if he would live throughout the night and waited before putting him through more surgery.

Later, I realized that he had recognized me; I had seen it in his eyes, but I did not know him. His ear had been partially cut off and sewn back on (a little crooked). The impact had broken his jaw; his swollen head looked ready to burst.

The fantastic thing is today, as we look back, we see that God had a plan for this brother of mine who had become an alcoholic. Hutch recovered from the accident, and it took a while, but he eventually returned to shrimping. Today he is retired and will tell you he serves a God who has shown him mercy. He lives in Georgia and works with the Gideon's, delivering Bibles and preaching in jails and prisons.

This "accident" is just another example of God working in our lives and teaching us how to live One Day At A Time.

6

OUR FAMILY CHANGES

OUR FAMILY WAS going to grow, and we were excited. However, it continued to be a rough pregnancy after returning from Texas. I threw up every day for nine months and lost from 127 lbs. to 85 lbs.

I went for my regular checkup on a Saturday morning (Yes, the doctor's office was open on Saturdays back in those days.) Jackie left me there while he ran his mother on an errand. I had not been feeling well, and my back hurt.

Finally, after waiting for what seemed like hours, the doctor came in with a big smile and said, "How are you doing today, Bonnie?"

I wanted to tell him, tired of being sick and throwing up every day, but I smiled instead and said, "I am fine, but my back is killing me."

I did not know what labor was like and was surprised when, after examination, he said, "You are in labor, so we need you to go on over to the hospital. I will be over a little later to check on you."

Jackie had timed it just right and came in as the nurse helped me into a wheelchair. He was nervous and excited as they pushed me out to the car. The nurses told him it would be a while, and if he wanted to get something to eat or had anything he needed to do, he had time.

He said, "I need to take Mom home, but I will be right back."

The doctor came in just as Jackie turned to leave, "You go ahead, we are going to be here a while. I have nothing to do, and I will still be here when you get back." Jackie stood there for a few minutes, hesitant to leave, and as he kissed me, Dr. J said, "She will be fine."

When he got back, they let him in once in a while, but they would only allow him to stay a few minutes.

My doctor, true to his word, came in to check on me off and on at the hospital that night, and on the following day, Sunday afternoon, October 4, 1964, Isaac Matthew Wise III arrived. A beautiful, happy 7 ½ pound baby, smiling from the first minute he arrived. Jackie was so proud and excited; you would have thought he had just given birth.

That is when he began helping me through it all; he fed Isaac, changed diapers, and helped clean the house. We became a team in whatever life gave us.

Richard and Lois, our close friends, had a daughter soon after Isaac was born. We spent time together at the beach and camping. We had a simple life, content and full of happiness.

Two years later, after a much more comfortable pregnancy, Daphne Dawn arrived on August 9, 1966. Our curly, dark-haired, blue-eyed, prissy little girl soon had her daddy wrapped around her little finger. She loved her frilly dresses, lacey socks, and jewelry.

Eventually, as the children grew, money became a little scarcer, so I started looking for a job. Living in Yulee, finding a job was no simple task. I worked on a chicken farm, and it is one of the nastiest, stinking jobs you could ever have. Perfume cannot even cover up the smell. It was hard to make the chickens get off the nest, pick up the eggs, put them in flats, stack them, and then carry the large stacks to a trailer that pulled them to the egg house. I still cannot stand to smell or eat eggs!

Yulee had one grocery store, IGA, and eventually, I became their cashier, which allowed me to meet most people in Yulee. Almost everyone came into the store at least once a week. The loggers would stop by early mornings for a coke, coffee, or to take a break for a few minutes. I met many people there who continue to be my friend today.

Later, I started working at Napa in Jacksonville, pulling parts and working on the packing line. That, too, was hard work, but at least it did not stink. Time goes by quickly, and eventually, we moved to Jacksonville because now we both worked there.

We continued to go to the beach, played games with the kids, played dodge ball in the street with our neighbors, and I had time to be the Cub Scouts Den Mother for Isaac. Daphne took tap and jazz, just a typical prissy little girl. We had a good life, but it was not without difficulties.

7

JOY AMID TRAGEDY
AND SORROW

WE STILL LIVED in Jacksonville when I received a call that my brother James was missing from his shrimp boat in Texas (July - 1970, Somewhere in the Gulf of Mexico). The crew went to bed, and he had stayed up to do some work on the boat. When they got up the following day, they found that the boat had not been anchored and was still running - James was not on the boat.

The Coast Guard and other shrimpers searched for him, but James' body was never found. My brothers and sisters all drove to Tennessee to be with Mom & Dad. James was my first sibling to pass away. He and Sonja had four beautiful girls, Pam, Alecia, Peggy, and Bib.

As hard as this was for our family, I can look back now and see that all of these things were a part of the teaching process God had planned for me. Our life seemed to be flying by, and now Isaac was in school and Daphne in Kindergarten. We had always planned to have one more child, but we had almost given up on having anymore and decided we would be happy with our two. All of a sudden, it started - morning sickness! So surprise!! We found out we would have an addition to our family.

Jarrett Jason was born on February 7, 1971, and he did not arrive small like the other two. He was a big baby and weighed 9 lbs. 2 oz. and was only 19 inches long. It didn't take Isaac and Daphne long to spoil their new brother. To Daphne, he was a doll, and she wanted to hold him. Three children made a difference in our house, and it seemed now we were busy all the time.

A short time after Jason turned a year old, we drove to Georgia to visit my sister Dean and her family. When we got there, we all went to Charlotte to see our sister Mary. She had been ill and was still not feeling well. She had two daughters, Barbara and Faye, who lived close enough to visit with them. We all had a great time that weekend and came home late on Sunday.

There was no indication of what was to follow, but I received a devastating phone call a few weeks later. My sister, Mary, had committed suicide. She died from a self-inflicted gunshot wound right through her heart. How do you handle that, as you see her husband and two daughters hurting? Seeing our Mom and Dad face a horror like that?

It is the Grace of God that gets you through all these times, and there have been many. Our life did not consist of one long, sad tragedy. We came from an average, loving, happy family.

We learned that God's grace is always sufficient, and He will never give us more than we can handle. We had a large family, a lot happened over the years, but we always faced every situation as a family together.

8

JACKIE'S ILLNESS

JACKIE'S FIRST SIGNIFICANT sickness occurred when we lived in Jacksonville while working for a Roofing company. He came home from work very ill one Friday afternoon. He did not like to miss work and always worked, even when he felt so bad he barely hold his head up. You never heard him say he was sick or feeling bad.

We had some mechanical problems with our car, and his brother Johnny came over that Friday afternoon to help him work on it. Jackie had a fever, but he refused to go inside and let Johnny work on the car by himself. He stayed outside with him and tried to help.

Later that night, after Johnny left, Jackie's temperature had gone up even more. None of the medications brought it down, and finally, I took him to the hospital emergency room. They found nothing wrong that would cause a fever. Nothing was showing on the X-rays, so they said it was probably only a cold. He had taken an antibiotic; his fever had dropped a little, so they sent him home.

Once we got home, his temperature rose again, and Aspirin

nor Tylenol did anything. It reached 104 and was still going up; I took him back to the emergency room. The last time they said he had a cold, and now after x-rays, they said he had a touch of pneumonia, and the coughing caused his terrible headache. They sent him home once again with a prescription for a different antibiotic.

The following day Johnny came back to help work on the car. Jackie was too weak to even get out of bed. His temperature stayed between 104 and 105 degrees, and nothing would help bring it down or help his agonizing headache. We had to do something, so I called my gynecologist, Dr. H.

I told him, "Jackie is very sick, and I know this is not your area of expertise, but I don't know what to do. His temperature has been ranging from 102 to 105 for the third day. We have been to the hospital twice, and they sent him home." I began to cry while explaining the high temperature, vomiting, and excruciating headache.

"Take him to St. Vincent's emergency room this time, and I will have someone there to meet you. You call me back if you have any problems."

We arrived at St. Vincent's, and they took Jackie back immediately and starting hooking him up to IVs. A neurologist came in to check him, then turned to me, "We need to do a spinal tap now. If you wait outside, they will let you know when you can come back in."

The emergency room had beds altogether in one extensive area, and curtains separated them. I stood outside the curtain, waiting. I only heard a slight groan as they did the spinal tap.

It only took a few minutes before they told me, "You can come back in now, Mrs. Wise."

His temperature continued to be high as I stood beside the bed and held his hand. The doctor walked back in a little while later. "The test results are back, but we cannot tell if it is spinal meningitis or encephalitis. We will need to do another spinal tap. We need to know which one it is so we can treat it properly."

Jackie squeezed my hand but said nothing. He continued to be in terrible pain.

The doctors walked out, and this time, they came to get Jackie and moved him to a sterile area to do the test.

I waited outside the little cubicle where he had been. When they pushed his bed back in after the second spinal tap, I heard them ask,

"I have Mr. Wise; Do you want him back in the same cube?" The next thing I hear is, "Oh, no, take him back out of here; he has encephalitis!"

Maybe I should have known what encephalitis was, but I didn't. We did not have Google, FB, and all the other social media or the internet. We did not have an education on all the life-threatening illnesses like we do today. Just the name was enough to scare me to death.

They moved him into isolation, and I had to wear a mask and gown when I went into his room. After several hours of testing and waiting, the doctor finally came back in.

"Should I call his mother since she is in Germany, and it will take her a while to get home?"

He replied, "No, he should start improving now that he is on the proper medications. The brain swelling will decline as his temperature comes down."

The nurse came in and said, "You can visit just a minute, but he needs to settle down now, get some rest, and let the medicine go to work."

Jackie looked terrible, but at least he could finally sleep. The nurse only allowed me a few minutes and then said, "You need to go home and get some rest. You look exhausted!"

It had been at least three days, and we had only a few hours of sleep during that time. I did not want to leave, but they told me they would call if anything changed. I could not stay with Jackie in isolation and visiting hours were over hours ago.

I left, and as soon as I pulled out, I had to stop at a red light. As I sat there, I thought, "Why am I waiting at this red light? Nothing is coming, and I can turn right on a red light."

As I proceeded under the red light, I realized I was not turning right; I turned left, which was how I needed to go! Thankfully, there is not much traffic. No police officer around, and I am on the way home after making an illegal left turn at the red light.

It felt good to be home even though I was worried, tired, and upset. I wanted to sit there and cry. I finally slept by continually reminding myself to slow down, take a deep breath, trust God, and take One Day At A Time. He is still in control.

Jackie remained in isolation for a few days; then, he spent several days in a regular room. Finally, he was ready to go home.

He was weak, and it took a while for him to get his strength back and eventually return to work.

They started looking for the encephalitis cause while Jackie was in the hospital and traced it back to his work. He worked for a roofing company, and it had been raining for several days. To give the employees some work time, they had all the employees clean up the shop. Jackie had been sweeping out the attic of their building, where pigeons had roosted. While sweeping without a mask, he had breathed in all the contaminated dust. The pigeons had passed on the encephalitis.

We later found out from his doctor, the first hospital we had taken him to twice had already had several encephalitis cases. They had failed to diagnose him, even with all the symptoms. Why? Only God knows, and He is still in control!

9

THE TEACHING ROAD

YEARS PASSED BY so quickly! I have read that "time and tide wait for no one"; this is so true. Time moves right on whether or not we are ready!

We moved back to Yulee because, after the first initial shock of living at the end of the Earth, it had always seemed like home.

I worked at Nassau Christian School and worked part-time at TG&Y, a small variety store, after school. We were still learning the meaning of living One Day At A Tim.

On May 31, 1982, we traveled down a road that would teach us many things. It was Memorial Day, and we were out of school, so I was at work at TG&Y when I received a call from Daphne.

"Mom, Daddy's home, but he is hurt, and he can't get into the house." Something was wrong, and he was in terrible pain. This is the same man who never complained about a headache, even with incredibly high temperatures, and never missed work.

"I will be right there." I left work and drove the 20–30-minute ride much quicker than I usually do.

He had gone to work at midnight, driving a Hess tanker with a fuel load from Jacksonville to Port Orange, Fl. He unloaded the truck, and when he bent over to pick up the hose, something happened in his back. The gas station staff wanted to call Rescue and have him checked out at a hospital.

He said, "No, just put the hose on the truck for me and help me get in. I can drive home." No one knows how he operated the brake, clutch, and gas for over two hours with all his pain. Only God could have enabled him to arrive safely back at the terminal. They, too, wanted to call someone for him, but no, he was going home.

He could only move a few inches at a time. When he moved, it was causing him excruciating pain in his back. When I arrived home, he was still trying to get to the steps to go into the house. I wanted to take him to the emergency room then. His reply, "No, I am going to take a bath first."

It took a while, but I finally got him into the house. Eventually, in and out of the shower, and finally, back down the steps and into the car.

He was exhausted and in extreme pain when we arrived at the hospital. They brought him a wheelchair to get inside, but he said, "No, it is better if I can stand."

So, he walked inside in intense pain, slowly eased into a chair, and then again refused a wheelchair and walked to x-ray. It hurt too much to bend his body to sit down.

Once in X-ray, it was another opportunity to wait. With each pain, he continued to break out in a sweat. When he had to stand, he either pushed on my leg or my shoulder, which allowed me to push him up with my weight when I stood. My shoulder and knee were bruised black and blue from the pressure, as were his knees.

The getting up and down at the hospital had exacerbated his symptoms and left him in excruciating pain. When it was his turn to go in for the x-ray, he said, "I can't go any further; I need a wheelchair."

They took him to his room and finally got the pain under control. Afterward, they tried physical therapy and everything possible for two weeks. He had lost about 20 lbs. during those two weeks, and he looked terrible.

He was always in extreme pain unless medicated; he finally told the doctors he was not going to physical therapy again. It was making his pain worse.

His back pain was in an area where the doctor assumed it was impossible to be a ruptured disc. The pain was only getting worse; he could barely move when, finally, the doctor did a myelogram. The results showed he had ruptured a disc; of course, nothing was ever simple. The doctor was excited because it was extremely rare for this disc to rupture. Jackie might be written up in a medical journal.

Jackie did not care about that; he just wanted the pain to stop. The surgery was scheduled and done with only a tiny incision in his back. The doctor told us he would be able to go home soon.

Isaac graduation

While he was still in the hospital, Isaac, our oldest son, had graduated from high school. Isaac came to the hospital in his cap and gown, so his Dad could see him. Jackie loved our children and was so proud of them. He had talked about Isaac's graduation for months and was looking forward to it. It hurt Jackie to disappoint them, but in this case, there was nothing to be done: Deep Breath, One Day At A Time".

10

PEACE IN THE MIDST
OF A STORM

THE DAY AFTER his back surgery, I was driving down Main Street on the way back to the hospital. I had to stop at a red light; as I glanced into the rearview mirror, a vehicle was coming toward me. It was approaching too fast, so I pushed on my brake as a van plowed into the back of our Ford Escort.

An elderly lady thought she was pushing on her brake but was instead pressing on the gas. When the van hit the car, I continued to press on the brake while praying I would not get pushed into the busy intersection. God is still in control. Our little station wagon now had the back bumper inside the wagon! It was bent and crushed but still drivable.

On June 15, 1982, the day after the accident, I had a doctor's appointment before seeing Jackie because my neck and back were hurting. While sitting there on the exam table, waiting for the doctor, I had an uncanny feeling my Dad was here. It sounds crazy, but it was as if he kissed me on the cheek. I just knew he was with me, telling me goodbye, and everything would be ok.

Dad's health had been up and down for several years, and several times, my sister, Tiny, would call and tell us they did not expect him to make it through the night. When we started arriving at the hospital, the doctor said he had never seen a man with such a will to live. It always seemed to give him more strength and pull him through. He had worked hard all of his life to provide for our family and was the greatest Dad ever.

I left the doctor's office the day after the accident, and when I arrived back at the hospital, Jackie said, "Dollbaby, would you get me some crackers?" I walked back to the lounge and got him some. Then, before I sat down, "Dollbaby, would you get me a coke?" I laughed and said, "Anything else while I am going?" He smiled, but it was not a smile, so I thought he must be in pain. He was in pain, but not from his back.

When I came back into the room, I reached for the phone to call a friend who had access to a toll-free line. She would call for me, check on my Dad, and then call me back to tell me how he was doing. There were no cell phones then. I usually only called from home because it was expensive to call long distance.

Jackie looked at me with tears in his eyes and reached out to hold my hand. "Don't call, Dollbaby; your dad just died." He did not know how to tell me, so he kept sending me to do something until he knew how to handle it.

I left the hospital in tears, driving my wrecked car, and smelling gas fumes, but I knew in my heart, everything would be all right. Going through the toll booth in my wrecked car with the window down, singing a song Johnny Parrack had recently sung at our church, "Peace, peace, wonderful peace, coming down from the Father above, sweep over my spirit, forever I pray with fathomless billows of love." They probably thought

I was crazy when I handed them my money with tears running down my face singing this song in my bent-up car. But I have learned God brings us peace during every storm if we only listen and wait on Him. It may be in the words of a song or in Scripture we have read, but our peace will be there if we trust Him.

During my drive back to the house, Jackie had called the church. Our pastor Bro. Larry and his wife, Ginger, who is also my best friend, were out of town. Our co-pastor, Bro. Bill Ford was there when I got home, and then friends arrived. We had not yet started getting workman's comp checks from Jackie's work, so we had no money; my car was all bent up, Daphne was at teen camp, and Jackie was in the hospital. So what was my plan? I did not have one, but God did.

Philippians 4:19King James Version (KJV)

[19] But my God shall supply all your need according to his riches in glory by Christ Jesus.

One by one, as my friends came to our house, they gave me hugs, some gave me money, but they gave me words of comfort. One friend offered me their new car, and he took my wrecked vehicle home with him. God again had supplied all my needs. Two of my friends, Glenda and Andy, came and were going to pack for me. I didn't have many clothes from which to choose. We wore a uniform to school, so Glenda went to her house, got her luggage, and packed her clothes for me to take.

Another couple came, and when they were ready to leave, he asked if it would help if his wife drove me. He also gave me $100, which was worth a lot more than it is now. I told him I had more than enough money, but he told me I might need it for something when I got there. I did; I gave it to my mother to help pay for my Dad's flowers.

I had a new car to drive, more than enough money for the trip, and a friend to ride with Isaac and me there. Francis did not go to the funeral but stayed at Mom's house and took care of everything there. She had all the food organized and ready for the family and friends who came by after the funeral. God is good and supplies all our needs In His Time!

My Mom and Dad had grown up in Tennessee, but he and Mom moved back when he retired in Florida. They were happy there and finally able to relax and enjoy themselves. I am sure it was not a simple task having to clothe and feed 11 children, but our home was a happy one. I never heard my Mom or Dad complain about anything. They were satisfied with the things we had, and Mom learned how to stretch a dollar a long way. We always had a clean home and home-cooked meals every day.

When Mom & Dad moved backed to Tennessee, it was as if they had never moved to Florida. He still had many friends and family there, and they came to see us and share their stories about him.

All of our family was there for his funeral. We did not get together often because we spread out between Florida, Texas, Georgia, and some in between. I barely spent time with any of them, but at least we were all there for Mom when she needed us.

I had to leave and come home as soon as possible since Jackie was still in the hospital. We had gotten there late the night before and left as soon as we had dinner with the family. A quick trip up and the stress of Jackie's hospitalization for a couple of weeks, it was a long trip home. I was very tired! Perhaps, exhausted describes it better.

As soon as I got to our house, I went straight to the hospital to bring Jackie home. It had been a few weeks since we were all at home together. He was in the hospital for three weeks.

Deep Breath and take One Day At A Time. We are a family, and we are all together again.

Part II

Our Lives Change

When Jackie was well enough to get around by himself, I went back to work at school. I still had my part-time job at TG&Y and now also at K- Mart. I had just found out TG&Y would be closing, and one of my friends had told me Amelia Island Plantation needed someone to work afternoons.

Here is where we see how God maneuvers each step of our life according to His plan. I had not heard of Amelia Island Plantation and had no idea where it was.

I applied for the part-time job at Amelia Island Plantation, which started me on an almost 30-year career path in hospitality. I look back now and see how God planned situations and circumstances in my life to lead me to where I am today. When we place an obstacle into an ant or colony of ants' path, they go around it or over it and move on. God does the very same thing in our lives because He knows the right direction for us. He leads, trains, and guides us to the path where we need to be.

11

GOD PROVIDES

JACKIE WAS OFF for two-and-a-half years, and God continually provided all our needs. It was challenging to work what had become two full-time jobs, but I had weekends off from both the school and Amelia Island Plantation. The weekends allowed me to rest before starting another Monday of an 80-hour workweek. Isaac had gone to college in Tennessee but came home and worked to help us out.

During this time, we also had two other major life-changing events in our lives. In 1984 Daphne graduated from high school and was married on August 10. She had her large, beautiful wedding, thanks to the help of our loving family and friends.

Isaac and Cheryl were married three months later, on November 10' and they also had a beautiful wedding. Again, we see how God has not just supplied our needs but has supplied above and beyond. He provided the desires of their hearts!

Jackie eventually went back to work but had to have more back surgery. The doctor explained this time; the incision would be on his stomach instead of on his back. If they cut him from the navel down, it would give them a better view of the front, where they were doing the spinal fusion. He also had an incision in his hip, where they removed bone for the fusion. The surgery was to take about twelve hours. Imagine our surprise when the doctor came out after six or seven hours, and the operation was successful. He told us Jackie, who had been on blood thinners for his heart, had bled very little so he could get in quickly to do the fusion and get back out.

After a prolonged recovery, the fusion healed, and he finally returned to work driving the tanker. However, there was more injury to follow. He went back to work driving the truck, and there was a spill. He stepped in it and fell off the top of his tanker truck. He tried to protect his back, so he twisted while he was falling.

The turn was successful, and he did not land on his back. However, he landed on his side with his arm stretched straight out. This position and the pressure from the fall caused some severe damage to his shoulder. When he fell, his arm was straight out, and I can only imagine the pain it must have caused.

Surgery repaired the shoulder and the rotator cuff. To say the physical therapy was painful is putting it mildly, but he never complained. He went back to work but insisted on pulling his weight and doing his job. The physical strain caused the muscle in his arm to fall. This muscle, of course, required another surgery. He had six pins in his shoulder. When he was well enough, he again started the painful physical therapy. Through these surgeries and heart attacks, he never complained.

I was the only one who ever saw in his face how much he suffered as the pain racked his body.

Deep breath, One Day At A Time, God is still in control.

12

HIS GRACE IS SUFFICIENT

AFTER MY DAD died, Mom continued to live in her house in Tennessee, and she had her garden, friends, and church. She came down and would stay with each of us until she was ready to go back home.

Mom had been here for a few weeks when she decided it was time to go home. The only problem was, my car was having some issues, so I borrowed Tina's car to take her home. (Tina was our new daughter-in-law. She and Jason had gotten married a few months before.)

When Mom and I left my house, Jackie walked to the car, kissed me, and told me to be careful. He was rubbing his left arm, so I asked him," Are you ok?"

"Yes," he said, "My shoulder is hurting where the pins are. It will be fine!" He walked over to the car, kissed me again, and sent me on my merry way.

We were driving to Jesup to spend the night with my sister Dean. She was going to Tennessee with us, so I would not have to drive back alone, and we would be two hours ahead on our trip. We planned to leave early the following day.

When we arrived at Deans, she was not there. We found her key, and as soon as we got inside, the phone was ringing. It was Tiny, my sister, who lived across the road from me. She said, "Bonnie, you need to come home. Jackie has had a heart attack."

Dean was home by the time I got off the phone. She said she would take Mom to Tennessee the next day. I left and got back to Fernandina Hospital a lot faster than I had gotten to Jesup.

After I had left to go to Deans and was out of sight, Jackie had gotten in his truck and drove to Tiny's house across the street. He walked inside and asked them to take him to the hospital. He thought he was having a heart attack.

He was extremely pale, having chest pains, and had all the symptoms of a heart attack. He never wanted me to worry, but I was ready to wring his neck because he let me leave. He thought the pain would pass, but it did not. It was a mild heart attack, and he was out of the hospital in a few days. Through all of Jackie's illnesses and accidents, he would always say he was "Fine," but I eventually learned if he was rubbing his shoulder or his elbow hurt. It was most likely a heart attack. Did he learn his lesson? Let's see!

Months later, Daphne and I were at church for a baby shower. The phone in the kitchen rang, and it was for me. It was Jackie, "Dollbaby, are you ready to come home?"

"Yes, but Ginger is sick, and Daphne and I were going to see her before we came home."

Ginger was my best friend, and he loved her. He was silent for just a minute, then said, "Do you think you can come on home?"

I asked, "What is wrong?" So, to my surprise, he says, "I'm having chest pains. Would you come home?"

I realized I should buy a race car or have a blue light on my car, but since I didn't have either of those, I called Tiny and asked her to go to my house and check on Jackie because we thought he was having another heart attack.

I waited a few minutes, and then I called. I was still a few miles from the house, and we had to talk in code so he wouldn't know.

I asked, "Is it his heart? Do I need to call 911?" So, this is the sister code here. She says, "Yes, I will stay until you get here, and Mike is on his way over." When she said yes, she was telling me I needed to call 911, and I did!

I had just gotten home and was walking into the bedroom when he heard the sirens. He gave me a look, the one which said that better not be for me. Tiny and I both acted dumb and said we did not call. He did not want to go with them, but we finally convinced him. He was having a heart attack and needed the attention they were giving him now. They were already hooking him up to everything and in touch with the hospital.

He always seemed to bounce back quickly and go to work, but the next one, the third heart attack, was different. We were driving, taking my niece home to Alabama, and then going to Tennessee to spend a couple of days with Mom. Now empty nesters. So, for the first time, a trip was planned for us, just the two of us. We would visit Mom in Cowan, Tn, first and then to Nashville for a few days. A trip to the Grand Ole Opry, dinner on the General Jackson, and some relaxing days at a lovely hotel–all complimentary.

We were almost to Birmingham, Alabama, when Jackie looked down and said, "Our alternator is going out."

Usually, this would not be a problem; it was something he could easily replace.

"I had to leave the toolbox at home; it wouldn't fit with all of Robin's things."

We made it to my niece's house, and her aunt told us she had a cousin who would do the repair work on the car. She had already called him and explained our situation, so we all got in the car to take it over to his garage. We stopped and bought an alternator for the car.

We were close to his garage when we had to stop at a red light. Yep, you guessed it, the car shut off and would not start. Jackie told me he would push it and turn left and go down off the hill. I tried to get him to let me push it, but he would not. I was worried as I looked into the rear-view mirror, but God had sent a good Samaritan who was helping Jackie push the car.

Halfway down the hill, I glanced in the mirror, and Jackie was still in the busy road, bent over with his hands on his knees. The good Samaritan was already gone. Jackie walked down the hill, and he looked as if he was having another heart attack.

I pulled over at the bottom of the hill and picked up the phone; the one in the big case zipped up! Guess what? They do not work unless your car does, and without a working alternator, your vehicle does not either.

I pulled over on the side of the road and jumped out of the car to help him. I wanted to send Robin and her aunt to find a phone, but he said, "I'm ok; I am just out of breath." Yes, he was out of breath and gray but would not let me call Rescue.

Her cousins came to fix the car where we had stopped. It rained, and Jackie stood out there with them while they replaced the alternator. He was in pain. The grimace on his face when the sharp pains hit said it all.

"Please let me get you to a hospital?"

"I will be ok," he said. "It is just my shoulder!"

No amount of talking could convince him he needed to go to an emergency room or to get out of the rain. Fortunately, it did not take long for the car repairs, and we left my niece and her aunt in Birmingham.

We started on toward Tennessee, but he did not drive far before he said, "I am going to have to stop and get some sleep. I can't go any further."

"Let's just go to a hospital," I saw the pain in his face.

"I'm just tired."

We stopped at the next hotel, and he continued trying to convince me he felt better.

After a restless night, we had breakfast and drove to Moms. (He later told me he thought he would die sitting there in the restaurant; his chest and arm hurt so badly. He was becoming an outstanding actor.)

We got to Moms, and we went to bed early, only to be awakened by the phone in the early morning hours.

My nephew, Jimmy, had an automobile accident and was killed. We decided we were going to stay Saturday night and come home on Sunday.

Saturday afternoon, as I helped Mom with some housework, I looked out the window where Jackie sat on the porch. He was gray around his mouth and having trouble breathing.

I opened the door as he said, "Dollbaby, do you think you can drive all night?"

I wanted to drive straight to the hospital, but he did not need to argue, so I replied, "I will try."

We left for the 12-hour drive to come home, and I almost made it all the way. I finally had to tell him, "I can't drive any further; I cannot stay awake."

"Pull over; I will drive."

He drove the last couple of hours. When he got off at our exit, I tried to get him to go straight to the hospital in Jacksonville, but no, "I am going home to take a bath, and then we will go."

He was weak, so I had to help him get his shower and then get him dressed. We finally got him to the hospital and his doctors in Jacksonville. He not only had a heart attack but had to have quadruple bypass surgery. His doctor could not believe the trip we had taken to get there. She told him that if he had to have a heart attack anywhere, Birmingham was probably one of the best places to have it with their medical facilities.

So, he had three heart attacks and quadruple bypass surgery. He had two pacemakers and, later, a defibrillator. He also had double hernia surgery, neck surgery, and three back surgeries. He did not just have two hernias, but two on each side. He had several operations and illnesses in his life - some major, some minor. He was a classic case of "You can't keep a good man down."

He came through each of them and went back to work as soon as possible. He was always happy and easygoing. He continued to help me at home with the housework, cooking and helping with anything we needed to do. We shared our tasks since we both worked. It was not my job or his job; it was our love, our home, our family, and our faith that carried us through the difficulties of our life. We had our family, a church family that was always there to help, and a God who never left us.

I had worked in Reservations at Amelia Island Plantation in the evenings while still working at school. I worked in Reservations part-time, filing paperwork, posting deposits, and mailing confirmations. While I was here, I learned reservations from listening to the agents while they were on the phone. I was still working 80 hours a week. I had the weekends off from Nassau Christian School and Amelia Island Plantation to recoup and start over on Monday.

When the time came, we knew Jackie would no longer work; I had to make a hard decision. I knew I had to take the Plantation position to make the most money and have insurance on the family. I had to quit teaching, and when I did, I cried every day as I passed the school on my way to the Plantation.

It was tough to adjust to all the changes, but God knew where I was needed and what I needed to learn. The lessons are sometimes taught only One Day At A Time, and that is how we have to learn them.

13

GOD GIVES US STRENGTH

JUNE 7, 1985, our 22nd anniversary, and we were spending our weekend at the Plantation. It was almost time for me to get off work, and Jackie was already at the pool villa where we were staying.

I gathered up my things to leave work when one agent stopped me. "Mrs. Bonnie, you have a phone call."

As soon as I answered, I knew something was wrong. My brother's family in Texas called to tell me my brother, Joe, had drowned.

A larger Shrimp boat had hit Joe's small boat, and it had capsized, trapping him in the cabin. He had drowned, but the Coast Guard had recovered his body. My nephew, who was asleep on the deck, was thrown overboard, and he had survived.

We again got together as a family and drove to Texas, this time for a brother's funeral. When something happens, I try to hold it together so I can help everyone else. After we arrived in Texas, I walked around alone, and then I went to the funeral home to check and make sure things were ready.

"Is my brother going to be ready?"

"If your brother is Joe, no, he isn't. We haven't started on him yet."

"Oh, no! My Mom is on her way and is going to be here soon. She will want to see him the minute she arrives. Why haven't you done anything yet?"

"The owner of the boat that had hit Joe's boat said his insurance would not cover it."

"What do you need?" I asked him. I did not want my Mom to hear all the issues about insurance or not be able to see him when she got there. They told me the cost of the funeral would be between $4 - $5,000.

So, I asked, "How long can you hold my check?"

"Two Weeks." He replied.

I said, "Ok, this check is no good for two weeks." I wrote the check and left to go back to my brother's house.

Jackie was in the living room with everyone else, and I sat there for a minute, then I leaned over and whispered in his ear. "I wrote a check for $4000++? Dollars" for Joe's funeral."

He just put his arm around my shoulder, hugged me close, smiled as he looked me in the eye to see if I was teasing, realized I was serious, and said, "OK."

He sat there for a while and then put his arm around me as he whispered, "Dollbaby, how are WE going to pay for it?"

Did you notice he said WE, not you? That was Jackie. I looked at him and tried to smile, but I couldn't. I just said, "I don't know, but I probably have 4 or 5,000 friends, and I will ask each one for $1."

It seemed like a good plan to me, but God had a better one. About a week after we got home, my sister-in-law called. She said, "The owner of the boat called to tell me his boat insurance was paying for the funeral." Then she said, "Can I just keep the check with Joe's things. I know how much you loved him."

"Of course, you can," I told her. I did love Joe and all of my brothers and sisters. They were and are all special to me.

While we were there for Joe's funeral, my sister Vivian (Bib) was not feeling well. She just sat in her chair with her legs pulled up into the chair. She didn't talk much, but I thought it was because she and Joe were close.

It wasn't long after Joe passed away that I received a call that Bib was hospitalized. I called her every day, and after all the tests, she had an inoperable tumor behind her heart, and she said that she just wanted to see my pretty smiling face.

She would always tell me how beautiful I was and pinch my cheek. I called her back after I had our ticket information and told her, "I will be there as soon as I can, but I have to wait until I get my incentive check to pay for the tickets."

We were going out there to be with her on December 7, Mom, Johnny, Dean, Tiny, and me. However, God had other plans, and she passed away before we ever got there. Mom had lost another child, first James, then Mary and Joe, and now Bib. I cannot even imagine how her heart survived all the sorrow she endured in her life. She was a strong little woman.

Bib had a funeral in Texas for family and friends. She was going to be buried in Florida next to a daughter who had died in infancy. I planned to meet Bib's casket at the airport and pick up one of my nephews who would travel with her.

Jason had a ballgame that night, December 7. I was there for a while, but I was sneaking out to go to the airport when my friend Ginger saw me leaving.

When she saw me walk out with Jason still playing, she followed me to see what was wrong. Jason had recently been diagnosed with diabetes, and when he was running and playing ball, it made his blood sugars go crazy. I was always at his games, and she knew I would not be leaving unless it was something important.

Ginger caught up with me outside. "Where do you think you are going?"

I didn't want to tell her, but she knew me too well, so I couldn't lie.

"I'm going to the airport to meet Bib's plane and make sure the funeral home is there to pick her up."

She would not let me go by myself. She drove me to the airport, and we waited for my nephew to come in, but he was not in the arrivals. He was supposed to be on the plane with her, but he was not there. I called the family in Texas, and he had missed the flight, but Bib was on it.

I asked everyone at the counters, checked with security in all the areas, but no one knew where she was. How hard can it be to find a casket which had just arrived on a plane?

Finally, we walked to the fence (before the days of tight security), and I looked through the gate, and Ginger finally saw it sitting outside. My temper flared, and I was so mad that they would leave her casket alone and outside.

We went back inside, and I tried to talk to them, but I was upset; all I could do was cry. Ginger had them call the Funeral Home to see when they were coming to get her. The day I was at the airport to meet her body was also the day we were supposed to fly out to see her. Why didn't we get to see her? I do not know, but God had a plan, and I try not to question why.

A few years after my sister Bib passed away, her youngest son, James, a few years younger than Jason, came to live with us. We didn't have him long, but we loved having him there. He brought so much into our lives. He was Bib's baby, so of course, he was spoiled rotten but adorable and thoughtful. He was and continues to be a blessing to us.

James has done very well and is married to Julie with a handsome son, Gentry. We loved him like he was ours and try to treat him like Bib would have. She would be so proud of him today.

Gene, my youngest brother, came home for Bib's funeral, and while he was here, his van tore up. It took him about three months, but finally, he got the van repaired and drove back to Texas.

Once home, he had to fly to Ft. Myers to captain a shrimp boat and crew back to Texas. Something happened, and they all disappeared between Ft. Myers, Fl, and Aransas Pass, Texas. No trace of my brother, the crew, or the boat was ever found. My Mom lost three of her children in less than a year. Only God can give you the Grace and Strength to survive the heartache. I hope I never have to know that feeling.

My sister Johnnie had been ill off and on for most of her life. She passed away, and later, my brother Richard had a massive heart attack. Now, Mom had lost 7 of her 11 children before her death on April 20, 2011. Her knees buckled as she walked down the aisle at the church after Richard's funeral. I thought we might lose her at the same time. Someone brought a chair, and she sat down and rested for a few minutes. Then, with a strength that came from somewhere else, she held my arm and walked on out to the car.

I have a video of her singing God on the Mountain. She believed every word in the song, especially the words "the God of the good times is still God in the bad times." Through it all, God has shown us He is still in control. Deep Breath, One Day At A Time!

14

IN GOD'S TIME

JACKIE HAD ALL his teeth pulled in 2003, and of course, it could not be simple. Nothing ever was. One had a root in the sinus cavity and had created an infection. I need to explain this for you to understand the trail on which our journey took us. The condition played a big part in his health in the future, but God knew, and this was His plan.

A few months after this, I accepted a Hammock Beach Resort position in Palm Coast, Florida. It was exciting to start on a new beginning with just the two of us.

It was hard to give my two-week notice at Amelia Island Plantation. I loved working there with the staff, guests, and owners. I knew the property, and the hectic busy seasons were my favorite times. Knowing every area of the Plantation allowed me to maneuver reservations around to make them fit and keep our guests happy. Our staff was excellent, and some of my best friends worked here. So, as excited as I was about the new opportunity, I was also sad about leaving a job, the people, and a company I loved.

During the two weeks of my notice, we went to Palm Coast

as often as possible to find a place to live. Nothing was working out for us to move. We could not find a place to live, and then, the final straw, Jackie, had to have a new defibrillator. I did not want to have any problems with his insurance because we struggled financially, just trying to keep our heads above water.

I finally had to tell Robin at Hammock Beach we could not come. With all of Jackie's medical issues, we needed to be sure he was ok before we made a move. We also had not found a house we both liked and was in a suitable location for work.

I finally told HR at Amelia Island Plantation that I would not move. They gave me a promotion for staying, but things had changed little after a year, and we knew we had to do something. Jackie's health had declined enough that we knew he could not work anymore.

I called Robin at Hammock Beach, and she told me the same position had become available. I had to reapply and come in for an interview. This time, in God's time, they were willing to hire me again after convincing them I would not change my mind again and would be there in two weeks.

After the interview, as we left Hammock Beach and came across the toll bridge, Jackie turned left instead of going straight to I-95 to go home.

"Why are we turning this way?" I asked.

He just looked at me and smiled, "If we are going to move here, I want to live on the water." We had looked all over Palm Coast the year before but found nothing anywhere we liked or could afford.

"Hey, there's a for rent sign," he said. We had both noticed it, and he turned onto the side street. The house looked nice, so we walked around it, looked in the windows, and called the listed number.

The owner said he was just around the corner and would be there in a few minutes. We fell in love with it. It was on a salt-water canal, just what Jackie wanted, with four bedrooms, three baths, and so much room. God provided not just what we needed but precisely what we wanted - in His time.

The first time I accepted the job was not in God's timeline. The second time, everything fell into place and worked out. Sometimes God says yes, sometimes He says no, and some-times the answer is to wait on Me, and I will make it better.

Our family and friends helped us to pack and prepare for the move. Keith and Allison helped us move down in his truck, and they all worked tirelessly to get us moved and settled. God is good to us, and He provided friends and family who helped us move into the house in Palm Coast.

The hardest part of moving was it took us away from our four children and eight grandchildren. I know it is only a little over an hour away, but it is more than the five minutes to which we were accustomed.

Isaac, Cheryl, Jenny, and Ian had just moved back from Tn, so they stayed and took over our house. God provided the home they needed.

Jason, Tina, Kristopher, Cassie, Daphne, Joshua, Jesse, and Samuel lived in Yulee. James, Julie, and Gentry live just a few miles away in Kingsland, Ga.

Once we had moved, they all came down often and spent the weekends. The grandchildren often brought their friends with them, and we always said the more, the merrier. We loved it there and had this house big enough for us, my mom to live with us, and sufficient room for our kids and grandkids when they came. They could fish from our dock, and we had kayaks and bicycles. Sometimes they brought friends with them, and they all had a ball, and we loved having them there. It all happened according to God's timeline!

Finally, we could afford to do what we wanted and not have to worry. We could pay our bills, and we had a decent savings account. The part of our story you need to know here is during this time, the infection in Jackie's sinus cavity was on and off. He should have already had surgery to repair it, but he never told me how bad it was.

We moved to Palm Coast because it was such an excellent opportunity for us financially. It was also here that God taught us another lesson on his care and concern for us.

Working in Palm Coast enabled us to pay off medical bills from all the heart problems and other illnesses Jackie had in the past few years. We could also assist two of our grandchildren in furthering their education. Jesse and Jenny had moved down, and both of them worked at the resort and took college classes in Palm Coast. I am thankful that God allowed us the opportunity to work and live there. We made new friends, and it looked as if this is where we would live until time to retire.

We loved Palm Coast and Hammock Beach Resort. I believe those five years were some of the best in our lives.

Little did we know the bottom was going to fall out. It was happening everywhere, and people were losing their jobs as the economy plunged.

We were also laying people off at the resort, and on April 20, 2008, Robin, the Director of Human Resources, told me the General Manager, Carlton, needed to see us in his office. She looked as if she had been crying, and I knew that they would lay me off.

I assured my friends Robin and Carlton. I still believe everything happens for a reason. It was only the grace of God that gives me the peace of knowing this. I did not understand why it happened, but I knew that God has a plan and a path for us. We may never know why things happen in our lives, but here is where we learned to trust God even more than we had in the past.

Romans 8:28 - And we know that all things work together for good to them that love God, to them who are the called according to [his] purpose.

I left work the day I was laid off. Instead of going straight home, I rode around for a while before I called to let Jackie know. I wanted to be sure I would not fall apart. With all of Jackie's health issues, the bypass surgery, and heart attacks, I did not want him to worry about anything. I couldn't help thinking, OK, here is where we are currently standing: no job, some money, but I am over 60... I planned to work here until I was 80, but now who will hire me? Oh, yeah, and don't forget my mom is in her late 90s and lives with us. Only God could have kept me from falling apart and worrying about losing my job since my job was our primary income source. I was amazingly calm as I called Jackie and told him I was on my way home. So, when he asked why I was getting off early, I told him they had laid me off. He, too, seemed to be calm.

We stayed in Palm Coast for a year, but I could not find a job. No one was hiring; I was overqualified. I think they were nicely telling me I was too old. We eventually moved back to Yulee in a neighborhood where Jason and Tina live. Daphne and Isaac are only a few miles away. James, Julie, and Gentry were living in St. Croix.

Jackie could not lift much, so to make our move back as smoothly as possible, we rented a 17 ft U-Haul truck. I loaded it by myself with a bit of help from Jackie, and he drove it to our newly rented house in Yulee. I thought if we moved a little at a time and put it up, the move would not be as bad, silly me. Moving is never easy!

Our sons, grandsons, and nephews met us in Yulee and un-loaded the truck. Keith brought his truck down to Palm Coast when we were ready to move all the other things, and Allison came with him. They worked along with our sons and got the truck loaded, and although Keith had moved us down in one truckload, he could not fit it in one when we moved back. It took another complete load. They all worked hard, getting us moved back and into our house.

I am thankful for what God does for us, even when we do not know what or why it is happening. It is incredible to look back now and see how God had led us back to Yulee so we would be around our family more. We had big Sunday dinners every week, and whoever was off work came.

Jackie was home all the time, so he took Kristopher, Cassie, and Ian to school and picked them up on days when they needed a ride. He was so proud of all his kids and grandkids and our great-grandson, Trenton. Not only did we have our three children by birth, but God gave us James for a few years, and then Julie and then our grandson Gentry. Sometimes we go through trials, but God gives us blessings and turns our sorrow into joy. I lost my sister Bib to an inoperable tumor behind her heart, but I am thankful we gained a son when her son James came to live with us.

15

GOD'S GRACE

I LOOKED FOR almost a year after we moved back before I finally found a job. It differed from what I usually did, but it was a job, and again, God is still in control, so who am I to question?

So, where are we in our learning? In Yulee, I am working for a Real Estate Company, and I work at a condo property office on the beach in Fernandina Beach, FL. My mom is living with us, so my sister, Tiny, came during the day, and she and Jackie took care of mom. Home health also came because it takes a lot of time and patience when taking care of someone who is now 100 years old.

We celebrated her 100th birthday with over 200 guests. My niece Terri decorated everything beautifully, and Mom had a wonderful birthday. She loved having company and seeing all her friends and family. We were a large family, six girls, and five boys, but now, there are only four of us left. Mom had lost 7 of her 11 children before her death on April 20, 2011. Through it all, God has shown us He is still in control. Deep Breath, One Day At A Time! I cannot imagine the pain and grief of losing one child, and here she was at 100 and had lost seven of her children and several grandchildren. Her eyesight is failing, but her mind is still sharp, and she can still tell us stories from her childhood.

Mom's 100th birthday party. Standing left Dean Tyre, Bonnie Wise, and Joy (Tiny) Kirkus. Seated: Hutch Shetters and Mom, Ethel (Judy) Shetters.

Mom continued to be more and more feeble. Some nights I was up with her 4 or 5 times, but I would not trade a minute of that time for anything. It was challenging since I had to get up each morning and go to work, but I imagine when I was a baby and cried during the night, it was hard for her to get up and go the following day.

We celebrated her 102nd birthday in February 2011, and she passed away on April 20, 2011. I had spent the night with her and was holding her hand when she went to sleep. She woke up during the night and put her hand on top of mine.

Tiny came, and she stayed with Mom while I left to go to our brother-in-law's funeral. I ran home, got a bath, and was on my way to the funeral so I could be with James and his brothers and sisters when my phone rang. It was Tiny telling Dean and me to come back to the hospital.

We had her funeral in Fernandina, and then we went to Tennessee and had another one for family and friends there. We buried her beside Dad; they were finally together. Once again, God has shown us His Grace is sufficient for all our needs. (II Corinthians 12:9 And he said unto me, My grace is sufficient for thee: for my strength is made perfect in weakness. Most gladly, therefore, will I rather glory in my infirmities, that the power of Christ may rest upon me.)

16

GOD'S PLAN

JACKIE HAD BEEN helping to take care of Mom, helping with chores at home, and doing all our cooking throughout the week. He still has a sinus infection, which has been on and off for several years. He also now has a chronic cough and has been spitting up blood. I finally convinced him to see Dr. Tribuzio in Fernandina. He referred Jackie to an ENT doctor for the sinus problems and sent him for a CT since the X-Rays had shown nothing.

He saw the ENT doctor who did a CT scan for his sinus issues and discussed the results. He wanted to see Jackie again the following week and asked him to bring me with him because we needed to make some decisions. I knew when I heard those words; surgery would be required. Because of Jackie's heart issues, I called Mayo Clinic and scheduled an appointment for him on July 5th. Jackie did not want to go to Jacksonville, but we had the appointment if he needed surgery, and he agreed to go. Again, here in this, I see the hand of God directing us to where we need to be.

Proverbs 3:6 King James Version (KJV) [6] In all thy ways acknowledge him, and he shall direct thy paths.

We made the return visit the following week to the ENT doctor in Fernandina, and he went over the surgery Jackie would need. I listened as he explained the operation. It would be at least a four-hour surgery to do all the repair and remove the cyst growing inside the sinus cavity. After hearing all the doctor had to say, I looked at Jackie and then the doctor as I asked, "Did he tell you about his heart condition?"

"No," he said, "He didn't. How bad is it?"

Three heart attacks and bypass surgery. He has had two pacemakers and now has a "defibrillator." I did not even mention all the other health issues.

"Well," he said. "This creates a problem."

My reply was to let him know, "Yes, it does, and because of all of his health problems, I think we need to go to Mayo." Little did I know the trail we were on and how this journey would end, but God knew, and it was all part of the plan.

Jackie finally agreed to go to Mayo, and I had already scheduled his appointment for July 5th. He just needed to pick up X-rays and CT Scans from his ENT doctor in Fernandina to take with him when he went.

I was at work at the condo property when I received a call.

"Hey, Dollbaby, I am going to pick up the scans from the ENT doctor and then going by to check with Dr. Tribuzio to see if my chest CT results are back."

Dr. Tribuzio was standing out front when Jackie arrived, so Jackie told him he was stopping by to see if the results were back. "No news is good news. I will check to see if the results are on my desk."

He returned shortly and told Jackie, "Have a seat; I need to talk to you." I wish Jackie had not been there by himself when he talked to Dr. Tribuzio, but God knew, and that is the way He arranged it. Maybe Jackie needed some time alone, or he just needed time to decide how to tell me. It would be like him to think of me first.

Jackie left Dr. Tribuzio's office and called me at work to let me know the results of the CT scan. I had barely said hello when he said, "Dollbaby, I have lung cancer." No casual, hello sweetheart, I'm on the way to see you. Just the words we had dreaded, lung cancer!

Talk about an eye-opener! We were afraid the results would be cancer since he was sometimes coughing up blood, but we were praying it was not. Even then, we tried to deal with the fact that we still did not know how bad it was.

Breathe deep and take One Day At A Time. Those words went through my mind so many times a day and in the year to come!

After he told me it was lung cancer, he said, "What are we going to do?" My very calm reply was, "Come to the office, and we will call Mayo." I then wanted to scream...... But I didn't.

When he got there, he was a little pale, and as he hugged me. I told him, "We will be ok, and we will make it through today, and tomorrow we will face tomorrow." We could only face One Day At A Time.

We then called Mayo to see if I could get him to see a pulmonologist, but they had nothing until September!

I knew he could not wait that long, so I called my niece, Robin. She is a Mayo nurse and is one of the sweetest, kindest, and most patient people you will ever meet. She is always the same anytime you see her, and God had placed her at Mayo.

Now, you may not believe that, but if you knew the incredible story of why their entire family moved to Yulee from Pensacola, you would see the hand of God in all our lives. Their move came because of much tragedy, heartache, and pain, but through His design. It is too painful for the family to discuss here, but God allowed her to be where she could help us when the time came.

Robin talked to one doctor there, a friend of hers, Dr. E., to see if she could help get her Uncle Jackie in earlier than September. Robin called back and asked me to fax the CT results to her, and she would show it to Dr. E., and then she would see what she could do to get him in.

Later in the afternoon, Robin called to let me know Dr. E. said if she could not get him in with a colleague on Tuesday, July 5, she would see him herself on Wednesday, July 6.

Here is where your heart beats faster, and you want to cry, but you remain calm and say, "That is awesome!" If Dr. E. would see him herself, I knew it was not good. She is an oncologist. **Deep Breath, One Day At A Time**! Do not think, do not worry, Trust God!

Jackie got an appointment to see Dr. J. On July 5th - the same day as the ENT appointment. See how God works?

I cannot say enough good things about Mayo. Everyone there was terrific. These staff members are the most considerate and caring people I have ever seen. During Jackie's illness, every involved department at Mayo and everyone who treated him was always compassionate and concerned.

We saw the ENT doctor first, and he looked over the CT results and concurred with the doctor in Fernandina. They set up a surgery date, and he, too, said it would be an extensive surgery. We left here and went to our next appointment with Dr. J.

Don't think ahead, don't worry, we will take it One Day At A Time. We are together, and we will handle it together.

17

GOD'S DESIGN

WHEN WE MET Dr. J. on July 5th, there was an immediate connection as far as she and Jackie were concerned. She was everything you could want in a doctor and a friend. She said on his first visit, as she checked his pulse:

"Would you be surprised if I told you that you are in AFIB?"

We replied at the same time, "No, it is like that all the time."

She told us we needed to put the sinus surgery and lung cancer on the back burner, and he needed to see a Heart Failure Doctor. I did not know there was such a doctor! I also learned there are many doctors I did not know existed. I began my new medical education while learning to live One Day At A Time.

As we waited outside in the lobby while Dr. J was setting up the other Heart Failure Doctor and the other appointments for him, we heard the scheduler tell other patients they could not get in to see a cardiologist until September. We looked at each other with the same thoughts, "We cannot wait that long."

Finally, the scheduler calls us up to go over all the dates, pages full of appointments. They begin immediately, and as she is going over the list for the next few days, she came to the cardiologist, and we held our breath as she said: "You have an appointment with the cardiologist–next Tuesday! How did they do that?" We just looked at each other and said, Thank You, GOD!

Luke 18:27 King James Version (KJV)

27 And he said the things which are impossible with men, are possible with God.

We did not see just one cardiologist but three heart doctors. Why three? This was the first question I asked the cardiologist when we saw him at the first appointment. This is how he explained it so I would understand: "If you are building a house, you have a contractor. He knows pretty much everything, but he calls in an electrician and a plumber to do the detail and specialty work."

Jackie now had a contractor, electrician, and plumber to deal with his heart, each one with their specialty. He had not gotten an appointment with one heart doctor, but three. Isn't God good? He had someone who looked at each area of his heart.

We focused on each day as we came to it, and not before. One Day At A Time was all we could handle. He saw many doctors and for two months had tests, blood work, X-Rays, and finally, they all agreed he could go ahead with lung surgery. They scheduled it for August 22 with Dr. A, a cardiothoracic surgeon. He was not only an excellent surgeon but one of the sweetest, kindest, and most caring doctors I have ever met. Jackie and the two assistants, K and R, soon became more like friends. I was always glad to see them because they cared so much about Jackie's health and recovery. The care was genuine, and if Jackie had tears in his eyes, they did as well. I have never seen doctors like these. God not only provided our every need but above and beyond. Every day-on time-every time, One Day At A Time.

The weekend before his surgery, Jackie had his 72nd birthday, and we celebrated at our Sunday lunch.

The operation was on all our minds, but we all put on a brave front and had a good time. We had almost all the family together. James, Julie, and Gentry were still living in St. Croix.

If I had known this would be the last birthday card I would ever give him, would I have chosen a different one? I do not think so. This card said what was on my heart at the exact time.

For my Husband

*Love puts the beauty
in everyday things,
the warmth in a home,
the joy in a memory,
the "we" in a dream.*

For My Husband

Love puts the beauty in everyday things, the warmth in a home, the joy in a memory, the we in a dream.

The older we get, the more I think about what really matters in life,

And so many of the things that once seemed important no longer even make the list.

What really matters to me now is the two of us, Sharing our lives, reliving our memories, Dreaming our dreams... together.

And your birthday seems like the perfect time to celebrate you...to celebrate us...and the joy of our life.... together,

I love you,

Bonnie

We were up early on Monday morning for his surgery.

<u>**Life was never the same after that day!**</u>

18

GOD'S PATH

FROM THAT DAY of his surgery forward, he was hospitalized every two to three weeks, sometimes in Fernandina and sometimes at Mayo. On the weeks Jackie wasn't hospitalized, we sometimes still had to go to Mayo every day of the week. God continued to provide and care for us in his time, and One Day At A Time.

But let's go back to the day of surgery: Jason, Daphne, Joshua, Jennifer, Tiny, Terri, Bro. Pete and Jackie's brother-in-law, Herbert, were all there on the day of his surgery.

Dr. A. came into the waiting area and took us into a private room to discuss the surgery. "It took a little longer than we expected, and the news is not as good as we had hoped it would be. Because of the cancers' location, we had to remove the entire right lung to get all of it and leave a good margin. The top lobe, which we had hoped to leave, had a different type of cancer. The cancer was also in three Lymph nodes, but the following four were ok. The "good" thing is they were close to the tumor in the lower lobe, which means, hopefully, it has not spread to any other parts of his body. He will need to see an oncologist and have treatments, probably Chemo, when he gets over this surgery."

Deep breath and pray, remember, our goal today was to make it through surgery, and he did. He is in recovery and will soon be in his room.

I looked at everyone and tried to smile. "Thank God they could get all the cancer. I know he will be fine; he always comes through surgery and does great. So, he will get strong and then have chemo and radiation."

The following words were posted on Facebook after surgery to keep everyone informed:

It was impossible to return all the calls as much as I wanted to. To all of you who have called and wanted to see Jackie but cannot, this picture is for you. He is doing great, as you can see. He is having a minor heart issue, but they have started him on a new medication. We are thanking God for his mercy, grace, and guidance.

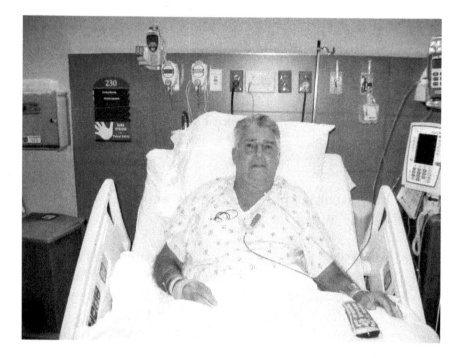

God gave us a feeling of peace, and we discussed the fact that many people live with only one lung. Even John Wayne made a movie, which finally won him an Oscar with only one lung! If possible, I knew Jackie, with his love of life and family, could do okay. If he continues to do as well as he has so far, we will go home by the weekend. It is only by the grace of God.

August 24, I noted Jackie had a rough afternoon after such a good morning, but he is feeling much better now. We slept for a few hours last night. He has already walked a little this morning and is only using the automatically administered pain meds. He has had little pain, for which we are very thankful. We should hear about the lymph nodes today or tomorrow.

August 27, On Tues. Jackie looked great, but he has gotten worse each day after, and today is extremely weak, still on IV, and throwing up. No bowel movement yet, so he does not feel like eating and is not getting stronger. We slept last night for about 4 hours straight. Please pray that soon, he will be better and start regaining his strength. We know God is able and does still answer prayer.

It was a rough time as he started recovery. He had to get up and down, sit in a chair, and walk down the hall. These things were so painful but had to be done to regain his strength. Finally, after one week, we went home facing **One Day At A Time.**

August 30, 2012, We slept in the recliners. He only took one pain pill since eight last night and one at three this afternoon. He is feeling much better, eating a little more, and doing great.

Home health was excellent and came to help us as he recovered his strength. We had a nurse, an aide, and a physical therapist. It looked as if things were going along great. He was walking with the therapist, looking and feeling good, getting better each day. We thought.

As soon as he was rested enough and feeling better, we had our Sunday dinners, and all the kids and grandkids who were not working on Sundays were there. I cooked now by myself, where Jackie and I had done all of it together before. It was not the same without him in the kitchen, even though Daphne, Jenny, and Cassie all come to help.

It was like my right arm was missing, but at least he was there. He loved it when they were all there, laughing, talking, and spending time together. He always got better when they were all home.

19

GOD'S BLESSINGS

I HAVE WORKED all my teens and adult life, sometimes at two or three jobs. I was off work for what I thought would be around six to eight weeks at the most. We have no substantial savings and no backup funds, so yes, we lived in today. Today, the bills are paid, and it is easy to say that God is in control.

God's Word says we are not to worry but to believe and trust God that He will take care of everything. However, I am the type of person who wants to do everything for everyone else, solve all the world's problems, and be the mother to everyone. So, how could I learn to wait on God? Have I learned?

My answer to those questions would be, I am still learning. It is a growing process, and I don't think I could have jumped into this. God has a way of easing us into our life's situations if we trust Him. So, how were we going to pay the bills, buy gas to run back and forth to Mayo, which is 45 minutes away, and, of course, Nanny Bonnie and Papa Jack did a few other things for the grandkids! How would we manage?

How does God prepare us? Gradually, He slowly equips us for the way He expects us to live — **One Day At A Time.**

Sometimes we do things and do not realize the effect they will have on us later. I had purchased a couple of AFLAC policies many years ago when I worked at Amelia Island Plantation. After I move to Hammock Beach, I added a cancer policy.

When I was laid off, it was sometimes harder to pay the premiums when they came due, so I started putting them on my American Express card. It was not always easy to pay the bill, knowing it was "something we could do without," but it was a way I could spread out the payment.

After the lung surgery, I filed the paperwork with AFLAC, and within a few days, we received our first check. To say I was surprised at the amount is not an adequate description! The money from this check helped to keep us going through a large part of his illness. God knew when we bought the insurance precisely when we would need it. I can't say enough about AFLAC and how they care for their customers. Everything was done quickly and easily, with no questions or complaints.

20

GOD'S PROVISION

WE WERE BEGINNING to learn the lessons of **Matthew 6: 25. Therefore I say unto you, Take no thought for your life, what ye shall eat, or what ye shall drink; nor yet for your body, what ye shall put on. Is not the life more than meat and the body than raiment? KJV**

Can I say this is easy? No, I can't. But I can say this; not once during this time of illness did we do without anything. Not once did we not have a big Sunday dinner for our children and grandchildren unless Jackie was in the hospital. Not once were our payments late, nor did we have to wonder if we had gas to go back to Mayo.

26 Behold the fowls of the air: for they sow not, neither do they reap, nor gather into barns; yet your heavenly Father feedeth them. Are ye not much better than they? 27Which of you by taking thought, can add one cubit unto his stature? KJV

The basic needs of a bird are not much different from our own. They need food and water, but they also need shelter to cover and protect themselves from the weather. They need a safe place to raise their family.

Most of you probably think birds eat very little, and it would be easy to feed them. In relation to their size, birds eat more than elephants. So, it is not just a little God is providing, but more food is necessary to feed the little birds. Why worry? God feeds them, and He will take care of all our needs just as He has promised in His Word. Birds don't gather and store up food for tomorrow, but God provides for them as they need it, or maybe we could phrase it another way and say God provides for them, **One Day At A Time!**

> **28 And why take ye thought for raiment? Consider the lilies of the field, how they grow; they toil not, neither do they spin: 29And, yet I say unto you, even Solomon in all his glory was not arrayed like one of these. 30Wherefore, if God so clothe the grass of the field, which today is, and tomorrow is cast into the oven, *shall he* not much more *clothe* you, O ye of little faith? KJV**

What is more beautiful than a lily in bloom? Here it also says a "lily of the field," not of the garden where it is cultivated, fertilized, watered, and tended with care, but of the field. It comes up on its own and lives on the elements of the ground. Whether cultivated and grown in greenhouses or fields like wildflowers, a lily has a beauty of its own. Here we are told that Solomon, who was the richest of men, was not arrayed like the lily. If God so loved the lily and the grass of the field enough to clothe them in such beauty, does He not love us even more?

Our heavenly Father knows our needs, and He will provide just as surely as our earthly father knows our needs and supplies them.

31 Therefore take no thought, saying, What shall we eat? Or, What shall we drink? Or, Wherewithal shall we be clothed? 32 (For after all these things do the Gentiles seek:) for your heavenly Father knoweth that ye have need of all these things. KJV.

He provides for us in ways about which we might not even think. I mentioned before about a friend and his wife who moved us to Palm Coast and then moved us back. He continues to help us and to be a blessing.

Another person came into our life, S, and the story of our friendship is also unique and special. I met him many years ago at Amelia Island Plantation. A young man who, along with his wife, had developed a Business Intelligence System we used at Amelia Island Plantation for our reporting. He and I immediately bonded and became good friends over the years. I usually saw him at least once or twice a year at the HUG and HITEC conferences.

Some of our younger friends had called me Mama because I was a little older than most others on our HUG Board. It was only natural that Sudharshan did the same, and I became Mama Wise. He met Jackie, and eventually, all of our family, and he fit right in! He and his family have been and are such a blessing.

When Jackie first had the cancer surgery, Sudharshan called and then flew up to see us. He spent Sunday with us and while there, he wanted to do something for us. He asked if we were okay financially or needed any money or anything. I told him no; we were okay, and so far had everything we needed. A few days afterward, he sent us a gift card.

I called him and thanked him but told him we were ok. He said, "I know you are and if you don't need it now, just put it up. It is there if you need it."

Knowing nothing about the Medicare Gap or doughnut hole, we were getting ready to plunge right into it a few months later. We found out we had to pay for all of Jackie's medication until we reached a specific dollar amount or until January 1. Cancer medicines are not inexpensive.

See how God works? A person I met at work over 20 years ago became a special friend to our family. He sent us just the right amount of money to pay for all the medicine needed when we were in the Medicare Gap. The amount of his medication during that time came to exactly $1000.70. We learned God would provide for us in His time and in His way—One Day At A Time.

You may say, I don't know anybody who would do that for me. I would have said that, too, if I were not focusing on saying it is not a problem today. Today we are ok, and tomorrow we will face tomorrow. I did not know a friend who would do that for me. I continued to say to Jackie, "We made it through today, and tomorrow, we face tomorrow! One Day At A Time." I am not strong, nor is my faith strong, but I knew if I worried, so would Jackie; therefore, I could not worry about tomorrow.

We focused on the issues and circumstances in our lives, one day at a time while learning and growing in our faith. We were learning to live one day at a time as we began to put our trust and confidence in God, knowing He would provide everything we needed – in His time.

33_But seek ye first the kingdom of God, and his righteousness; and all these things shall be added unto you. KJV

Here we are told how this is to be. "Seek ye first the kingdom of God, and all these things shall be added unto you."

How do we seek the kingdom of God? Seek means to look for, search for, try to find, hunt for, or ask for. We are to study God's Word diligently to learn of Him and His righteousness. Then all these things shall be added unto you.

Take therefore no thought for the morrow: for the morrow shall take thought for the things of itself. Matt. 6:34 KJV

Don't worry about tomorrow. How do we do that? Well, this brings me back to our story and the lessons we learned. I pray that they will be a blessing to you.

21

THE ILLNESS CONTINUES

EARLIER, WE DISCUSSED that the lung surgery is over; we are home. We thought we were making headway in the healing process.

The first week went very well, but Jackie felt tired going into his second week at home. He was having night sweats and occasional fever, vomiting, and unable to eat.

Jackie continued to feel worse daily as his blood pressure was range was from 80/48, 91/50, and 85/60.

The pacer lab called and said it appears something is wrong with one of his leads, but it could be the machine. She just wanted to let us know. And they would look at it when he comes in on the 26th. I told her about his blood pressure, and she said, "He can't wait that long; bring him in tomorrow at 1 pm."

He is now eating very little and is too tired to get out of bed. He looks terrible.

Remember the sinus surgery on the back burner? We are

trying to get well enough to have it done. So, we take him back to see Dr. A., his cardiothoracic surgeon. The Physician's Assistant, K, is there, and while we are sitting there, Jackie is so weak he can barely sit up in the wheelchair. K says he will need a chest x-ray to be sure everything in the lung cavity is ok. Jackie looks at me as if to say. I am too weak; there is no way. He is exhausted and just wanted to lie down.

As all this is happening, Dr. A. walked by the door, and when he saw Jackie, he came inside. K. told him he was going to send Jackie for a chest x-ray. K. and Dr. A went outside and into the room next door. K. returns and tells us the doctors had met for just a few seconds, and Jackie needs to be admitted. First, we need an x-ray and blood work STAT! OK, now I am worried.

They explained that when the lung was taken out, the cavity fills up with fluid, which is the body's way of taking care of it. They were concerned he might have a bacterial infection in the fluid that was now in the lung cavity.

Daphne is in the waiting room. I had to ask her to come with me today to help because I was almost beyond going. It is so hard to hold him up, get him bathed, shaved, dressed, into the wheelchair and then into the car, put the wheelchair into the trunk, drive 45 minutes to Mayo, then get the wheelchair out and him back into it, push him inside the door, park the car, walk back to the building and then push him to the doctors. So thankfully, she is here and waiting for us.

K tells the nurses Jackie needs to go to get the work done STAT, but she wasn't sure how to get to the location. K said he would take him and was off in a run. As I am running to keep up with K, we go past the waiting room, and I called Daphne to come with us.

It only took a short time to complete his blood work and the CT scan. Then they drew fluid from his lung cavity for testing and finally took him to his room. He was frail, weak, and sick, continually throwing up. We were there for nine days. I say we because when he went into the hospital, I went in, and I did not go home until he did. He always wanted me to be there with him, and I would have been nowhere else. There was a sleeper sofa in the room, but I slept in a recliner. I turned it so that my feet were at the head of his bed, so I could hold his hand without twisting my arm, and I could see his face. It was hard to see him losing weight and sick, but we took each day as it came, **One Day At A Time**.

It is now September 12, 2011, and Jackie ate an egg sandwich, half of a blueberry muffin, and half a banana. He did not throw it up and dosed back off to sleep. We were still waiting for the endoscopy results and the biopsies and continued to pray he would get better.

It was hard to see Jackie continue to be frailer every day. They did not know why his white count was elevated. He has a bladder and urinary tract infection, but not enough for the high count. He has less stomach pain, has not thrown up, and we are now waiting on blood tests to see if his white count has come down any.

In a week, he only kept down a few bites of what he ate, and even the water he drank was thrown back up. He needed to get healthier for chemo and radiation, which should come up in a few weeks.

Jackie got weaker with each day as the nausea continued, and his blood work was now showing he was malnourished. He was frail, and his white count improved but remained high. Jackie had every kind of doctor imaginable and every type of test; they did a CAT Scan and chest X-rays. He had Infectious Disease Doctors, Doctors of Internal Medicine, and had taken almost every antibiotic available. He was still nauseous and continually throwing up.

My niece Terri was visiting Jackie during this time, and three of his doctors came in. One of them said: "Well, we have done almost everything. The only thing left is a brain CT to have a complete workup." As soon as these words were spoken, one of them was already putting notes into the computer scheduling the Brain CT. They went outside, and three more of his doctors came in. In less than 10 minutes, he had seen six doctors, was scheduled for the Brain CT and the stretcher was there to get him to go for the test.

As they move him onto the stretcher, the phone started ringing, and it was Dr. A. asking to speak to Jackie.

I told him, "He is on a stretcher going out the door on the way for a brain CT."

Dr. A. said, "They need to bring him back to the phone now." They brought his stretcher back in, and as Jackie took the phone, Dr. A. asked, "Would be you be willing to let a neurosurgeon do acupuncture to see if it stops the nausea."

I was very skeptical, but Jackie said, "I am ready to try anything."

He could keep nothing down and was losing weight quickly. They took him for the Brain CT and as soon as he was back in the room, the Neurosurgeon was there. I have seen nothing done so quickly and with such care and concern. It was amazing to see the teamwork between these physicians.

The neurosurgeon came in with a small bag, which he unzipped, and pulled out several needles. He placed these needles in various locations, from Jackie's head to his legs. These needles were attached to a widget with batteries, which would produce a light electrical shock for ten minutes. The doctor turned off the lights so that the room was dark. I could stay in the room, but I could not talk so that Jackie would relax.

The doctor walked outside for ten minutes, came back in briefly to check on him, and then went back out for ten more. He returned, removed all the needles, and looked at us as he said, "If I have done this correctly, there will only be one drop of blood on his wrist."

He pulled out the last needle, and one drop of blood rolled out of that little hole.

Jackie had no nausea after that for several months. Here again, we saw how God had a man there to do what was needed to stop his nausea at just the right time. He had only recently returned from Asia, where he had learned acupuncture. I don't understand acupuncture or how it works; I am just thankful that it did. We continue to thank God and live One Day At A Time.

September 16, 2011 (Email to Kim at work) Well, we are still here and do not know what has caused all of this. They are now looking at the pocket of infection in his sinus cavity, which the ENT Dr. does not think needs to be drained, but the Cardiothoracic team thinks it does. He has been off some of his heart meds because of the various effects on his body's other areas. Today they are trying to get him back on these meds. It takes a specialist to figure when and what medication he needs based on his blood work. They have also talked to the head of the ENT department and discussed his case with him. They are concerned about this infection.

He had acupuncture from a neurosurgeon yesterday for his nausea and has not been sick since then. The Dr. said this morning that throwing up is not a problem with most people, but it can be fatal to a person with one lung and a diseased heart. I am thankful that they took the chance and allowed the neurosurgeon to do the acupuncture. We know he is not going home today or tomorrow, but hopefully soon. Yesterday was a week, and it has been a long one. Mayo is a wonderful place, and I cannot say enough good things about them, but we are so ready to go home. Tell everyone we miss them and thank you all for your prayers.

Each day brought a new and different experience. We faced what came up this day and left yesterday behind and did not begin tomorrow until the sun came up again. **One Day At A Time** was all we could handle.

I can't remember every detail of his stay, but he had a very rough nine days, and the doctors were very concerned. They never determined the exact cause of all his problems, but this visit to the hospital started the downhill slide that we never could stop.

It was here that we genuinely focused on making it through today and trusting God for tomorrow. **One Day At A Time** had become our way of life and our words to each other every day. Let's make it through today, and tomorrow we will make it through again! Do not worry ahead of time about what may or may not happen - Wait on God! Deep Breath.

22

WAITING ON GOD

9/17/11 - FACEBOOK update: Jackie is going home today. He needs to have another surgery but not today; we trust God and focus on taking One Day At A Time. We will have a few rough months ahead, but God is in control and has provided us with a wonderful family and friends. We love you and thank you all for your thoughts and prayers.

We were finally able to go home for a couple of weeks for Jackie to regain strength for the sinus surgery. He was weak but could get up and down, walk to the living room, and eat some soft foods. It felt so good to sleep in our bed, in our house. There was no nurse at midnight, no blood techs at 4 AM, and no doctors at 6 AM every morning.

He could see friends and family more now that he was home. Mayo is 45 minutes away, so he did not have many visitors when he was there. Of course, once we were home, we continued to have our Sunday Family Dinners. Jackie looked forward to the time with the kids, grandkids, and anyone else who stopped by at mealtime. He loved having them all there laughing and cutting up even though he could not join them. The bedroom was open so he could see into the kitchen, and they had to pass by the door to get to the living room.

September 21, 2011 (Email to Bubbles) Jackie is extremely weak. He goes back to the Dr. on Friday and sees the oncologist on Tues. I don't know what the plan is, but we will find out on Friday. They are going to check the fluid in the lung cavity and do cultures on it. Hopefully, it is still ok.

September 27, 2011 (Email to Sudharshan) I just wanted you to know we had a better day today. The oncologist made Jackie feel better about the outcome of everything, but she said he needs the Sinus surgery first and then the chemo. She is worried if he gets an infection there, the chemo could make it worse. He is a little stronger today and ate an excellent lunch on the way home. I have everything in the house I can find that says High Protein.... now, if I can get him to eat and drink it! He has to gain some weight back and get stronger to go through the surgery. He has lost 29 pounds, but I told him not to worry. I have it in storage for him. I just need somebody that can do a fat transplant! The doctor told him a milkshake every day, my dream diet. Milkshake and ice cream!

We still have a long way to go, and chemo will probably make him sick, but if it gets rid of any cancer cells, three months of being sick are worth it. He will have this surgery on the 12th (it is a 3-4-hour surgery), and then as soon as he is strong enough, they will start the chemo. IVs one day a week for three weeks and one week off for four rounds, so four months.

Dr. B was the first doctor he saw at Mayo, and he set a date for Jackie's sinus surgery. He explained the surgery and told us how long it would take, but all this had to wait until now. Hopefully, he was over the sickness and gaining a little weight back. We now had a new surgery date.

The surgery was extensive, and it took almost the same time as lung surgery. Dr. B did the sinus surgery, removed the cyst, and repaired the drainage that was causing the infection. There were some issues with his heart, and they had some trouble waking him up. (One thing I didn't find out until later was they nicked an artery, and he lost so much blood that we almost lost him. Lack of blood flow also caused the surgery not to heal, and he could not swallow or talk because it also caused a paralyzed vocal cord.) We spent only one night in the hospital and went home. He ate some soft foods, primarily liquids, and was very careful with the incision inside his mouth. Focus on today only; tomorrow, we will face tomorrow. One Day At A Time.

October 13, 2011 (Email to Ferne in response to her email asking me about coming to work in November) We are at Mayo today. He had his surgery yesterday, and we are still hoping to go home today. Once again, we are waiting to see if his kidneys will work, so they will let us leave. It was a long day yesterday and a long night last night. I am so ready to get out of here and go home.

They took Jackie yesterday at 11 AM and finished around 4:30. The Dr. was trying to get all the cyst out (He said it was huge), and in the back, it was hard to get into the side of the cyst and the skin. In doing this, he cut an artery, and it took a while to get the bleeding stopped. He needed several pints of blood, but they will build him back up with vitamins. Not to mention, he is in AFIB most of the time. He could not breathe in the recovery room (later found out they had cut an artery, and he almost bled to death), and they had to call in some other doctors and put IVs in both ankles. His face is enormous on one side because it is packed. They will take the packing out on Monday. Hopefully, he will be well enough in a couple of weeks to start chemo, which will take four months.

I would love to work some (and need to), but he cannot stay by himself yet. He is frail, and sometimes I can run to the grocery store and leave him with someone, and he is ok. Jason and Tina were there last Sat, and I ran to the store. When I got back after about 45 minutes, he was in bed. Jason had put him to bed because he was too weak to sit up any longer.

Let me see how he does next week, and I will try to let you know then. Unless he improves a lot this week, I don't know how I can, but I may be surprised.

I miss all of you and am looking forward to coming back soon.

Part III

God Is Still In Control

Jackie was always such a trooper and tried hard to do what he could to get well. It was heartbreaking to push him in the wheelchair because he hated to be in it, but it was way too far to walk. You could see his health failing each time we went. He could not eat, unable to talk, but he still tried. Home health, physical therapy, occupational therapy, and speech therapy worked with him, but he continued to lose weight. We were on a downhill slide and no way to stop, but we continued to live only in today, expecting each day to be the one when he would finally get better.

One Day At A Time and Remember God Is Still In Control!

23

FACING TODAY

OCTOBER 13, 2011 (Email from Kim) Bonnie, Ferne, updated me on the progress of surgery and stuff. My prayer for both of you is a break, just a simple break. A break to breathe, sleep, relax, and whatever else your heart desires. I wish he would get through all this so he could start his healing and recovery. You are in my thoughts and prayers, and I know somehow, in all this, God is still sovereign.

Let me know if you need anything.

October 14, 2011 (Reply to Kim's Email)

Thanks, Kim, We finally got home last night around 7. Jackie was doing very well from this surgery and said his grits and eggs tasted good today. I am thankful for every slight improvement. Jason told him he looks like the dog Droopy in the cartoon with his jaw hanging down and swollen. He is in his recliner asleep now, but we slept better last night than we have in a long time. God is so good to us; I could not even tell you what he has done in our lives over the past few weeks. Thank you for your thoughts and prayers; I hope to see you soon. Bonnie.

We returned for Dr. B to check the incision, and he seemed to be okay. The doctor's assistant asked to look at it since she had never seen this surgery. With the doctor's approval, she looked in his mouth and said she did not see any stitches. Dr. B came over for a closer look, and all the surgery had come undone. I don't know who was more upset, me, Jackie, or Dr. B. He said it had never happened before and was probably because of his arteries and the lack of blood flow (from the cut artery). They were also checking his thyroid, even though last week it was fine. He will have surgery next Wed at 6:30 to repair this. It should only take about 30 minutes, so at least it is not as bad. They need to clean it out, cut until it is clean again and sew it up with thicker sutures this time. I guess this is also the little push where things continued to go downhill.

Jackie now has a paralyzed vocal cord and cannot talk. There was drainage from an open area from the sinus through the gum. The drainage was because all the repair work had come undone.

He had to be careful when drinking, or the liquid would come out of his nose. Later, the food or drink would go into his lungs, causing pneumonia.

He was on liquids and losing weight every day. I looked for every way to keep protein and vitamins in him. I found a Carnation Breakfast with 560 calories and 22 g of protein. I added peanut butter and ice cream to it. Anything to help him gain weight and have a little more energy. It seemed like we took one step forward and two steps back. He drank FSR Energy Drinks. If it was supposed to help, we tried it. We tried everything! He wanted to get well for us so badly, but it just wasn't meant to be. We stayed positive and didn't give up. He had the best attitude, and even when he felt his worst, he tried not to let us know.

10/20/11 Jackie had his surgery redone yesterday, and he is doing well. He has lost down to 183 and is on a liquid diet for ten days. He sees his cardiologist tomorrow, and we are hoping he can get the AFIB under better control. Once he gets over this surgery, he should be ready for chemo.

. . .

10/24/11 Back from Mayo, and the stitches from the operation last week are still holding. He is still really weak, but we are pushing the protein. Hopefully, he will do the chemo in about three weeks, and he will have some of his strength before he starts it. I am praying the worst is past, and we are moving toward recovery.

. . .

10/31/11 Jackie Update: He needed to be admitted today but begged off until Wed. They will put in a feeding tube to help him gain some weight, and the surgery will begin healing. He cannot eat and has been on a liquid diet, which cannot provide what he needs. He also needs more blood and oxygen to that area to help it heal; he may go to a hyperbaric chamber. His white count is up again, and they will do a battery of tests and scans to see what is causing it. He is weak, frustrated, and tired of being sick. He has some excellent, compassionate, caring, and capable doctors, and we are praying they find the problems and get them fixed so he will get healthier and well. We just need to make it through today.

. . .

11/2/11 Jackie Update: Thank you for all your prayers. Jackie was very upset about the feeding tube, and God answered his prayer. He does not have to go in today. He has been drinking a Carnation Drink with 560 Calories and 23 grams of protein twice a day. They will check everything on Monday. Please pray it will all be better; he will be stronger and start getting well.

. . .

11/5/11 Jackie update! He has gained 1.3 pounds in three days. He is drinking 560 Calorie Carnation drinks 2 or 3 times a day. He also just ate three pancakes and a few bites of scrambled eggs. We have to be careful about what he eats with the incision in his mouth. And this was a lot for him. He looks so much better than yesterday! Talk about opposites. We feed him as many liquid shakes as he can hold, and I just started the Body by Vi 90-Day Challenge (thanks to my grandson Josh). Jackie also has a Vi shake since it has so many vitamins & nutrients. We are praying he is on the way to recovery. He will see his doctor on Monday.

. . .

11/8/11 to Kim

We just got home from Mayo. They told us to bring a bag in case he needed to stay, but we are back. The incision has not healed, and the hole is there, but the stitches are still in. The gap may or may not close, but they need the incision to get well now. He needs to start chemo around the 22nd, which is three months from lung surgery. He has an antibiotic to take and one to use inside his nose as a wash. His white count is still up a little over 12000 but down from the over 19000 last week. He will see the disease control doctor as soon as they can get him in, probably tomorrow.

I will let you know.

24

GOD REMINDS US

Nov 17, 2011 Good Morning Kim,

We were on our way out the door to the doctor when my cell phone rang. It was the doctor's office calling to let us know he had emergency surgery. Can we come tomorrow? Sure, we can, although we got up early, rushed around to avoid all the traffic going to Mayo, got Jackie ready, labored to get makeup all over this fat face, and now I must do it again tomorrow. As I was helping Jackie change shirts, I realized how thoughtless and selfish I was. The doctor had emergency surgery, and some family is going through a struggle right now. I am just a little frustrated because our appointment is changed — It is time to get my priorities in order and pray for this family and the doctor today. I don't know what surgery he is doing, but I know he is a cardiothoracic surgeon, and if it is an emergency, someone is not doing well. (He is also on the transplant team, so someone may have even died for this surgery to take place.) God knows, and God knows our hearts. Lord, forgive me when I whine; I am so blessed.

The Infectious disease doctor just called (another reason we love Mayo) and wanted both of us on the phone. Of course, we feared the worst, but it was all good news. There was no infection in the fluid from the lung area they took out on Tues. and no bacterial growth on the cultures. He and the ENT doctor have given the ok for chemo, dependent upon the other doctors and the oncologist. It will be three months since his surgery on the 22nd, and that is when she wanted the chemo to start.

I think we may be on the way to recovery. He is still weak and out of breath, just walking to the car and back in. I want him to get healthy and be able to breathe easily. He is gaining weight. It is comical at mealtime. I am on the ViSalus shakes to lose weight, and he is on 560 calorie shakes to gain weight, so at least we are saving on groceries.

. . .

11/24/11 HAPPY Thanksgiving! We are truly blessed with family, and God is good to us. All of our needs have been provided, the turkey and ham are almost ready. The pies, granny goo, and sugar-free brownies are all done. Fruit and Watergate salads are made, and all the other holiday treats are just waiting for the rest of the family to get here for lunch. It has been an incredible year, and God has brought us so far. We miss Mom today. She loved the holidays when everyone was home. Family is precious; treat them as such and treasure every moment you have together. We wish you A Happy Thanksgiving today and every day.

. . .

11/30/11 Jackie has his first chemo tomorrow at 2:30 for 3 hrs.; we are taking a movie for him to watch. We are not sure how it will affect him yet, but we expect God to take care of him as He has so far. He has gained a little weight and looks much better. We are praying chemo doesn't make him sick, but if it does, that is a bridge we will cross tomorrow. Please continue to keep him in your prayers.

. . .

12/1/11 First round of chemo behind us. Thank you all for your prayers. Jackie did great, and we just got home; he ate and is taking a power nap. He is probably down for the night, but he said he was just taking a nap. We'll see!

. . .

12/2/11 Email to Kim - We finally made it! Jackie started chemo yesterday. He looked better yesterday than he has in months. He has not been sick yet since they gave him meds before the chemo. We will know soon how it will affect him or if it does. He has two different meds for nausea if he needs it. We already have meds if he gets sick in the middle of the night or on the weekend and needs antibiotics. They have tried to prepare us in advance for anything that may come up.

He cannot straighten up or walk very far, but he has improved so much, and we are thankful. His appetite is growing, and he has gained back some of his weight. I will get him a hat to keep his old bald head warm when he loses his hair. All the boys said they are shaving their heads when Papa loses his hair. I will make sure we have a family photo!

I am hoping I can come back to work soon. I am not sure when and won't know until we are a little further along with chemo. I will keep you updated. Hope to see you soon.

12/4/11 Jackie is still very ill, despite two types of nausea pills. He has lab work at 9 in the morning, and they are putting in a port at 2 pm. It will be a long day tomorrow. Pray, he feels better, or he won't make it to Mayo. He has an appointment every day this week but Friday. He has to feel better.

. . .

12/5/11 My gray hair has turned my brain blonde; today, I was rushing to get the car to pick up Jackie out front after putting in the port. SOOOOOOOOOOO, before we start a 45-minute ride home, I went to the lady's room. I went into a handicap-accessible stall so I could put my laptop on the sink. Did you know that the automatic water will turn on for a computer? I hope it dries out. If you don't see me on here after today, you know it fried!

. . .

12/12/11 Email to Kim, I talked to Ferne Sat. Jackie has only had one chemo treatment. Last week his blood pressure was extremely low, and the nurse had trouble finding a pulse. She looked at his lab work, and the potassium was at a dangerously low level, so they gave him an IV and Potassium and antibiotic for two hours. We went today for lab work and a Chest CT. We also stopped by to see the ENT doctor, who did his mouth and sinus surgery. He wasn't in, but we could see the Nurse PA. On Sunday, Jackie was having some sinus problems, and when he talked, sometimes you could not understand him. Today when she checked him, he has a sinus infection, and one side of his vocal cords is not moving. She had no idea why or how long it has been this way or if this is something new.

He is a little depressed. I try to stay positive, but sometimes it gets hard when we go to Mayo; it is always something different and totally out of the norm. We got his top dentures redone with the added piece to cover the hole in his gum (which is bigger now than it was before surgery). We will need to redo the bottom one because his teeth have shifted, and the wires on the partial no longer fit his teeth.

We go back tomorrow for another round of potassium and a liter of the IV fluids because he is dehydrated again this week. I am not sure when he will get more chemo. I guess we will find out tomorrow. Make it through today and face tomorrow - tomorrow. One Day At A Time.

. . .

12/17/11 Jackie update: Sorry I have been slacking in the updates. He has only had two chemo treatments. The first one caused him to have low potassium, which resulted in low blood pressure, so he had to skip the second chemo for a week. He had it on Monday and has done better with this one. He also has a paralyzed vocal cord, which is affecting his speech.

Some days are better than others, but we are praying he will continue improving and growing stronger every day. Thanks for your thoughts and prayers.

25

IT'S THE LITTLE THINGS

12/26/11 Email to Sudharshan

I didn't want to say Merry Christmas, and Jackie is not doing good in the same email. For the last three days, he has primarily been in bed, but he got up for a while yesterday and ate a little. He was up today for about 30 minutes, ate a small breakfast, and went back to bed. The chemo is kicking his butt. His body hurts; he gets nauseated and has no energy. I started to take him to the hospital on Christmas Eve but finally got some fluid in him at home. The chemo makes him cry a lot, and he apologizes because he can't do anything. It is hard to see him like this, and I keep reminding him this is only for a couple of months, and then he will be all over it, and he will feel better. He weighs 176, but I know that he will get back to normal when he gets over the chemo. He looks so bad, but I put a couple of pictures on Facebook from Trenton's party so you can see how he looks. My niece, Terri, came over last night, and when she saw him, they both cried for about 10 minutes.

Daphne is doing good; she has tears and cries when she leaves. Jenny tries to cheer him up when she comes by after her classes. She sits by him, and he hides her M&M in the compartment between the recliners so nobody else eats them. The boys try to be tough, but it's hard for them too. I have to remind all of them; the medication (the cure) makes him sick, not cancer. They got all the cancer, and he will get better. He sleeps a lot during the day, so he wakes me up a lot at night. I guess I am going to learn to nap when he does until he is well. They gave him a new med for nausea but won't fill it until tomorrow when they make sure the doctor wrote it. Evidently, it has pot in it, and that will help his nausea and appetite.

Kristopher (Jason's son) went to put gas in Jackie's Jeep for me and backed into a mailbox; he called me crying and so upset. I told him a broken taillight, and a few scratches on the car were a small thing in the grand scheme of life. He wasn't hurt, and neither was anyone else. So, as you can see, our life goes on, and it is these little things in life that make us appreciate what we have.

God has blessed us beyond measure with our family and blessed us by adding you to our lives. We love and appreciate you! Hug my grandkids for me. I hope you can come to see us when you slow down a little. I know you are busy, so I will be patient. Just don't wait so long they forget me. Who knows, when Jackie is over this, we might make a trip to see you. I have my house upside down. The Christmas tree is down and packed, and now I am going to clean. I had better get busy, or he will be up.

Love you & Sherry, take care, and I will let you know how Jackie is. He did not have chemo last week but has a double dose on Thursday. We are praying it doesn't make him any sicker.

. . .

To: Sudharshan Wednesday, December 28, 2011, 9:39 AM

We didn't get the new meds yet. We are still waiting for the pharmacy to call the doctor. We see her Thursday, so we will have her call if not by then. He had a good day yesterday. He ate more and stayed up almost all day. He wanted a Krystal burger, so I had Kristopher get him some, and he ate them and has kept them down. He had to go to bed about three times for a little while, but he seemed stronger and talked better. He drank an energy drink, FRS, supposed to be suitable for Chemo patients, and I don't know if that did it, but as soon as he gets up this morning, I am giving him another one. Hopefully, he can drink it today.

Love you, Mom

. . .

1/1/12 Sudharshan

Good Morning and Happy New Year!

I just wanted to let you know that all of Jackie's blood work was good on Thurs. Everything was in a healthy range. He had his double dose of Chemo and is doing well so far. Every other treatment is two different medications, so it is pretty strong. No nausea yet!

He will probably lose his hair this week, so I bought him a couple of little pull-on things to keep his head warm. His head is small, so he looks funny with them on, but I will get used to it. He is staying optimistic, so it is a good thing. If he has lost more hair this morning, we will probably shave it. Who knows, it may not all come out.

1/6/12 We had a good Christmas, even though Jackie was in bed most of the day. He would get up and then go back to bed when he got so weak and tired. He had another chemo treatment yesterday and has been up more today than he has in weeks. It affects him differently from day to day, but he is doing very well, considering all they have done. He is half-way with the chemo and back down to 174, but all his blood work looked good this week. He has home health coming to do physical therapy, so he will hopefully be stronger soon and walking better. He can make it from the bed to the living room, and once in a great while, he will venture out to the mailbox. He came to open the door for me today when I locked myself in the garage, and the door wouldn't go back up (don't ask me why). I thought I might be stuck out there, but he heard me just before I turned green and was ready to jerk the door off.

Take care, and we hope to see you soon.

26

FACE TOMORROW - TOMORROW

Jan. 11, 2012. Finally, we have internet access. Jackie was admitted Monday night with pneumonia, which is a little rough with only one lung. He had chemo last week, his immune system is down, and he is already exhausted without pneumonia. Jackie has lost all the weight gained, so we are back to square one. Overall, he is doing some better, and hopefully, we will go home tomorrow or Friday. Please keep him in your prayers.

. . .

1/12/12 Email to K

Jackie had his fourth chemo yesterday. He is halfway now, finally. He has been in bed for most of the last couple of weeks and is exhausted. They come to do physical therapy with him at home two or three times a week, depending on his Mayo visits. We only had to go two times last week, and hopefully, we are off all next week unless they call us. He was up for a couple of hours today but is back in bed now. I hope the PT will help him get healthy, and he will move around better.

They will bring him a walker next week since he can only walk from the bed to his chair. He lost some weight and is back down to 174, so I am trying to fatten him back up again. We pray he gets better soon. His next chemo will be the week after next, two weeks on and one week off.

. . .

Jan 15 Jackie was admitted again and is better today. He may go home tomorrow or Tuesday; he had two units of blood, so his counts are up but still low. He is supposed to have chemo again Thursday, but I think his counts may be too low; I will wait on that one. I am just glad there is an improvement. I am ready to go home. He could only have four chemo treatments before he got too sick to go on. His counts dropped too low, and he had to have a blood transfusion. He was ill and had to take antibiotics. He was put back into Mayo with pneumonia.

We dealt with it all by saying we made it through today. Tomorrow we face tomorrow — One Day At A Time.

. . .

Jan 17, 2012, Jackie is home. He can only whisper because he is weak, but I am sure he will get stronger now since we are home. His blood work is looking better, so the transfusions are working. Since he has heart issues, he is in heart failure, but this is not anything new. He ate breakfast and had physical therapy at 12, so he is one step toward getting stronger. We continue to concentrate on One Day At A Time. Thank you for your prayers.

. . .

Jan 25, 2011 Email to Sudharshan

Hey, How are you doing? I thought I would give you a Jackie update. We went to Mayo yesterday, and they have stopped the chemo since it is causing many problems. We came too close this last time to losing him. The doctor said we have no guideline to tell us that eight treatments are enough or six, five, or four. We also don't know if it will come back. His quality of life is what we had to look at, and he could not go on like he was. The chemo just brought him further down each time he took it. He has lost 50 lbs. (while I have gained). I hope we can reverse this trend, and I can get skinny, and he can get fat. We have a nurse and physical therapist coming to the house to help him exercise and regain his strength. The blood transfusions have brought his levels all backup, so everything is almost back to normal. They should continue to get better since he is not having chemo destroy them all every week. He is a little nauseous now, and that is the first in a while. I will be glad when it is all out of his system. We go back tomorrow for a follow-up with the surgeon, and then I think our visits will slow down a lot. It wears him out to go down there. We love you guys. Hug the kids for me! ☺ Keep us in your prayers.

27

THERE'S NO PLACE LIKE HOME

IN THE FOLLOWING weeks and months, he was in the hospital in Fernandina and at Mayo. The rescue unit could not take him to Mayo since it was too far, so he went to Fernandina because he needed help quickly. Once, we paid out of pocket to have the private ambulance take him to Mayo. He had such an excellent attitude through all of this, and we continued to believe he would get better. He had such a will to live.

I am thankful that God has allowed me to come through storms and be able to adjust my sails. I am adjusting many sails these days, but confident we will make it through.

March 16 Jackie Update: We had an awful scare yesterday and had to take Jackie to Fernandina hospital. I thought we would lose him, but after spending the night and getting some fluids, he is home and doing so much better. It's hard to believe he could be so sick yesterday and so good today. We are thankful God has given him back to us, and we are fully trusting he is finally on his way to recovery. The pictures posted on Facebook recently were taken in Aug. He is now 70 lbs. lighter, a little grayer, but just as good looking. I hope our next update will let everyone know how fat he is and how strong he is getting.

Please continue to pray for us as we continue our journey, One Day At A Time! We are so blessed to have such a wonderful family, and thank God for them all. Yesterday was hard on them as we all waited here at home for rescue and then at the hospital. God is good!

. . .

March 19, 2012

I want to say a special thank you to Terry and Arlene for coming down from Asheville, NC, to spend a few days (not enough) with us. It was good for Jackie to have them here and have Chef Terry make him omelets for breakfast. I don't yet understand; I made him one today, and he did not eat it, but he ate all the ones Terry made. What's up with that?

Sudharshan flew up to spend a day with us. I thank God for the special friends we have made through the years. I genuinely thank you for all the calls and emails showing Jackie how much you care. We are trusting God that Jackie will soon be up, and well, then he can tell you himself... until then, Thank you!

He had pneumonia and was in Fernandina hospital, went home for less than a week, and was back in Jacksonville at Mayo. He was there for ten days. During this time, he had a feeding tube put in, and they had done three bronchoscopes to suction out his lung. By now, he had lost 70 pounds and could barely move on his own. Dr. M was taking care of him, and he loved her. She was so kind and always concerned. She did everything possible for him, and we tried so hard to get him well.

Their decision was at this point; he needed to go to a Rehab facility. The only way we would agree was if we could both stay because I would never leave him. They finally found one in Jacksonville close to Mayo. He can now only travel by ambulance. The place was beautiful to look at, but when we were in our room and night came, I felt like I was going to suffocate. I honestly thought I would have a nervous breakdown. I told him I was going outside for just a minute.

I tried to think about breathing deep and trusting God, but I was tired; I just wanted to go home. I know he did too. I called Daphne and told her, "We cannot stay here. Call Tiny and home health and get everything he is going to need. He needs to be home where he can see everyone, and he will feel better. I know it has to be as depressing to him as it is to me, and he will not get any better here. We can take better care of him with all of his home health. We are coming home tomorrow!"

I had seen no one from home in several days, and I knew we had to get closer to home. I talked to the staff the following day, and I told them we were going home. They advised against it, but I felt like he would get better care at home where he could relax and be in his surroundings, see family, and have a schedule suited to him.

Since we were leaving against medical advice, we again had to pay for a private ambulance to take him home. I did not care and would have carried him all the way. We had to go home, and we did. By the time we got there, Tiny and Daphne had a hospital bed and everything we needed. Home health care came and set up his schedule for physical, speech, and occupational therapy. They came and taught us how to hook up the feeding tube and give him his water and food. I had a journal of his water times and food times to keep it all straight. I wrote the time he took his medication since he was now on blood thinners (Somewhere along the line; he had gotten a blood clot in his arm.) It was only God who allowed me the calm in the midst of all the storms. One Day At A Time, when I needed Him the most, He was there.

. . .

Facebook Post: April 13, 2012: I just want to update our FB friends on Jackie. He spent 11 days in Mayo and then was so weak they encouraged us to put him in Rehab. We stayed there one night, and he wanted to come home, so we did, against their advice. He was now weaker than before; he couldn't stand or walk, even with help. We had to have an ambulance to bring him home.

Because we have such a loving family and friends, he has had company and lots of encouragement. I want to let you know that by the Grace of God, he is stronger, can stand, and could say a few words. He is still weak and has a long way to go, but he got out of the uncomfortable hospital bed and into our comfortable bed with no help. Stop by for a visit; he would love to see you.

He was weak and barely able to get out of bed, but he did whatever we all asked him to do. He wanted to get better for us, and he tried so hard. He could walk from his chair to the couch only about 7 or 8 feet, but it was like a mile to him, and he could just do it when the therapist was there to hold him up. He had the feeding tube and was gaining weight, and for the first time since August, he was hungry and wasn't able to eat. He could not swallow and still had the paralyzed vocal cord. Speech therapy came, and with her working with him, he could say a few words we could hear. She let him eat yogurt and pudding while she was here and had a little machine hooked to his neck. He started clapping his hands for me if I was not in the room, and he needed me. We would laugh about it because he expected me to appear like magic as soon as he clapped his hands, and I tried my best to do that. It looked as if things were finally getting better - Deep Breath, One Day At A Time.

Dr. Tribuzio came on Thursday to see Jackie at home and was pleased with his progress, expecting him to be much worse.

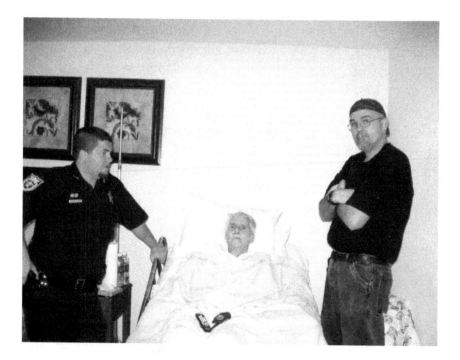

Jesse and Jason came by today to help get Jackie moved up in the bed. Sometimes my back needs a rest, and I just can't pull him up, even with the extra sheet.

During the following two-week period, God allowed some close friends, Lucille & Glenn, to visit us and spend some time with Jackie. It is a full-time job to take care of someone when they are in this condition, so Lucille came to help. I could not have made it through those times without the help and prayers of all our friends. I am so very thankful for the people God put in our life through the years.

When Lucille left, my best friend, Ginger, came from Tennessee, and it was so good to have her here. She said, "Ok, I am here to help you, so what do you want me to do?"

I told her, "The physical therapist just told me he is getting drop foot, and he needs to exercise it as much as possible. Your job is to make sure he is exercising his foot every time you walked by the room."

So, she did, and we just knew he was on his way to recovery. She helped me with everything while she was here, and all too soon, her two weeks were almost up, and she would go home in a couple of days.

On Saturday, Jackie had problems breathing, and we had to call Rescue to take him to Fernandina. The ER doctor admitted him, but we did not get to our room until 4 AM. We were exhausted by then. Ginger went back to the house to sleep, and I stayed at the hospital with Jackie.

28

IF I HAD ONLY KNOWN

HE SEEMED TO do better, and on Monday night, he slept with a pap machine to help with his breathing. I never left him when he was in the hospital, but he was doing much better on Tuesday morning, so I asked him, "Would it be all right if I run to the store and pick up some clothes so I can take a shower. Ginger will stay with you, and I will just run there and right back."

I had not had a bath since we had come in, and he was feeling better. Usually, he did not want me to leave him, but he shook his head and whispered, "OK." He was okay with Ginger there.

I kissed him and said, "I won't be gone long. I will be right back."

I was gone for maybe 20/30 minutes, came back to the room, and had a quick shower. Ginger waited until I showered, and Jackie was doing fine. He was not having any breathing problems or pain.

Ginger left, saying, "I will be back in a little while." She was having lunch with her grandson.

It felt much better to have clean clothes, and my hair washed. Reaching for Jackie's hand, I sat down in the chair next to him. He was lying very still, just watching me. I smiled, sat down, leaned over, and kissed him.

I picked up his hand, he looked up at me, and I realized then how much he had swollen in the short time I had been gone.

I thought if we could get him up, maybe some swelling would go down. The nurse and respiratory therapist were in his room, and they helped me get him up. He could help us just a little, but he was ready to get back into bed after a few minutes. When we tried to help him get back in bed, he was totally limp and had no strength. We had to put him back in the bed physically with no help at all from him. He was completely limp.

I put the C-Pap back on him as he looked at me and whispered, "I can't breathe."

I was facing him, and they were behind him, hooking everything back up, and they assured me the machine was helping him to breathe.

I looked at his face, and I told them, "He can't breathe!"

Since I was by his side, I reached up and took the C Pap mask off because I could see his face and knew that he could not breathe.

He reached up with all the strength he had left and put his swollen hand on my arm. I tried to help him, and as I looked into his eyes, he said, "Please." I knew what he was asking. His eyes said it all as he looked at me. He was weak, frail, and tired of fighting for every breath. He was asking me to let him go. How could I? He was fine just a little while ago. I did not want to let him go; he had fought so hard to live and had come this far. I was holding his hand, and when I looked into his eyes for what became the last time, I saw the pain, all the hurt, and I knew I had to let him go. So, I shook my head, yes, and whispered, "OK."

He closed his eyes, just as if he had fallen asleep. He was tired, he was ready, and God took him home. He was finally at peace and out of pain.

I've wished a million times I had not left him, even though it was just a few minutes. I would never have left him had I known it would be his last few minutes on Earth. He was doing better!

We never know the day nor the hour our loved ones may leave us, and I realize there is no way I could have known. Nevertheless, I wish...

Ginger later told me that while I was gone to get the clothes, he kept moving his head and looking up toward the TV, like he wanted her to look there. We believe his angels were there to take him, and he wanted her to see them. I know he was ready, but I wasn't. Nothing will charge you more than watching someone we care about die and knowing we are looking into their eyes for the very last time.

Posted on Facebook - May 1, 2012: Thank you all for your prayers. Our hearts are broken, but we know Jackie is not sick or weak anymore. I know we face some tough days, but I also know God will take care of us through it all. His favorite song was "Look for me at Jesus Feet," so that is where he is tonight. Please keep our family in your prayers.

Posted on Facebook - May 3, 2012: Thank you all for all your thoughts and prayers. It is good to hear from everyone. I sometimes log on, and then I try to answer all the postings because each of you holds a special place in our hearts. It is too hard, so please don't be offended if I can't reply individually. My heart is not just broken; it is shattered into many pieces. I love you all and thank you so much for your love, support, and prayers. Most of all, thank you for loving Jackie; he was an exceptional individual who loved his friends and family. I will post the obituary when they have it finished, but it will be at Oxley Heard in Fern. Friday 5-7 and the funeral on Saturday at 11.

29

EVERYTHING CHANGES

KNOWING HE WAS ready to go has given me the strength needed to go through these last two months since his death. It has been challenging, but God has held me up through it all, and I know Jackie was ready. I know where he is, and there is a song he loved, and he always told me when I get there to look for him at Jesus' feet. If he has the capability, I know that is where he will be.

He asked many years ago to have Danny sing this song at his funeral, and he did. Look for me at Jesus Feet was the perfect one for Jackie. I know where he is today. It doesn't mean I don't miss him because I do; every day, he is in my thoughts. I remember how he looked so much better than he had when he was alive and suffering. I can also tell you planning his funeral was the hardest thing I have ever had to do when you have a love like ours. The pain is suffocating, but you must go on. There are things only you can do, and you have a family that hurts when you hurt, so you put on a front for them and then fall apart when you are finally alone. Our children and grandchildren were strong, we all loved him so much, and everything changes when the family is no longer all together and never will be again.

So many friends stepped in and helped during and after Jackie's funeral. People God had put in our lives in the past—for such a time as this. Cindy, Brad, Darlene, and I don't know who else took care of food, set up tables, and had everything at home ready when we got there. Keith and Allison were there and always were through all of his struggles.

Some G.I.R.L.S. I graduated high school with came and spent the day, Bubbles, Patt, Charly, Jeanne, Glaconia, Joanne, Elaine, Sandy. I'm not sure who else was there; I just can't remember. We didn't get to talk or spend much time together, but they were there if I needed anything.

Sherry flew up and stayed all day with me, but Sudharshan was out of the country. Cindie, Robin, and Madeline came from Hammock Beach; it meant a lot to me that so many of our friends stayed to be there with us. Carlton came but had to go back after the funeral.

God helps us through days like this and even at the viewing. I do not remember everyone that came, although they talked to me; I believe this is just God's way of allowing us through the pain. He knows how much we can handle.

30

TRUSTING GOD IN OUR LIFE AND OUR LOVE

THE FOLLOWING ARE posts from Facebook since his death. Our love was one that some people only dream of having, not that we had everything, but that we had each other. When you trust in God, things are different, and in trusting Him, we learned the walk of how to Live and Love, One Day At A Time. God allowed us the time we needed to give him up. Even though it is still hard, we knew it was time, and we know where he is.

God is still God and always in control. He knows what we need, and I often remind myself these days to make it through today and then make it through tomorrow, One Day At A Time. It is hard, and some days I cry off and on all day. I lost the companionship and the love of my life after 49 years. He never failed to tell me he loved me when we talked on the phone or when I left the house, or just because he wanted to. He told me how beautiful I was, no matter how bad I looked. I miss him so much. Some days I make it through and don't cry at all. It can be a song, a word, something he liked to eat, or something he didn't want to eat. I try to breathe deep because it is hard to cry when you are taking a deep breath. It doesn't always work, but I say to myself, "deep breath: One Day At A Time, One Breath At A Time."

God has repeatedly proven that He is in control, and He will take care of us. Just as I relied on Him to provide for us all those months, I rely on Him today. If He held my hand during all those hospital stays, He will continue to hold my hand day by day as I continue to learn to live "One Day At A Time."

Update: June 2012

It has continued to be hard to live where we lived and see the places he sat, stains from spills, and just any little thing that reminds me. When I could finally try facing work again, I found out that I could work part-time for July and August and possibly at another location after that. After two meetings, I was told to let them know when I could go back to work. I was to have my old job again after some review and go over any changes that had taken place while I was off. I called the office to let them know I would work part-time while looking for another job, but no one ever called me back.

God is good. My bills are paid, and I have a trip to Ireland and England in September, a gift from friends. I am looking for a full-time job, and some terrific friends at Hammock Beach are trying to find a job for me. I have three part-time jobs. I continue to live One Day At A Time, which is how God wants us to live. I want to be in God's will. Please pray for me as I endeavor to live <u>One Day At A Time.</u>

31

A SPECIAL TOUCH FROM GOD

I AM NOT sure the date I wrote this, but it was during a time in my life shortly after Jackie died when I felt like I not only lost him but my family as well. His death differed from the other ones we had faced together in our life. Everything changed when I lost Jackie; the way I ate, what I watched on TV, and even our friends changed. I was living a totally different lifestyle. It was changing daily, and I learned that death affects families in different ways. It seemed as if ours fell apart for a while. Some came over; some didn't. I understand that it is different when someone you love so much isn't there anymore, and going where they lived is hard. Remember that no matter how you are related to anyone, it can never be as hard on you as it is on the spouse. There is no way to describe the pain and heartache adequately. I have an entirely different way of life that I didn't want, but then, I remember that God is in control; He has a plan for me, and He will provide.

This Scripture got me over the biggest hurdle in my life, and I realized no matter bad your pain and sorrow, no matter how much someone hurts you, we need to get over it and go on. I also know it is only God who can pierce your heart with His Words.

When I wrote these words, it was only for me, but today, as I reread them, I hope they will be a blessing to you as well.

Psalm 102

First, here is a brief history of where I was in my life on this day when I read Psalm 102. Jackie had passed away on May 1, 2012. My heart was broken, but I tried to stay strong for everyone else in the early days after his death. My tears were in private when I took a shower, went to bed, or when I was alone, and then my grief consumed me. I cried until all I could do was sob myself to sleep. I felt like I was going to suffocate. There are no words to describe the grief, the pain, the loneliness, or the heartache you feel.

Then you second guess your decisions and ask yourself, Could I have done more? Why did I do this, or why did I do that? Am I the reason so many things are happening now with the kids, the grandkids? Did I say something wrong at dinner on Sunday? What should I do about the house, the car? Where are they? Why don't they call? Did they love their dad and not me?

Grief is not for just several days, and then you are over it. I don't know that I will ever get over the pain and heartache of Jackie's death and all the surrounding circumstances that have torn my family apart.

When I started reading the first verse of Psalm 102, my heart broke because I felt as if these very words came straight from my mouth. I felt God's presence as I read:

1. Hear my prayer, O Lord, and let my cry come unto thee.

Sometimes I prayed and felt that it was not going anywhere, like God was not listening. When I read this verse, it was like a prayer going straight into God's ears. I knew that He heard these words. I cried, and I knew that just like the words in verse 1, God listened to my prayer, and my cry had reached His ears. It was as if my weathered heart, like a sponge, had been filled with water and was being squeezed, cleansing my heart and soul as it released the water through tears from my eyes.

2. Hide not thy face from me in the day when I am in trouble; incline thine ear unto me: in the day when I call, answer me speedily.

3. For my days are consumed like smoke, and my bones are burned as an hearth.

Please, God, don't hide your face because I am in trouble. My family is in trouble. Please hear me and answer my prayers.

My days go by so swiftly, just like smoke from a flame. It is here, and then it is gone. Life on Earth is short.

4. My heart is smitten and withered like grass; so that I forget to eat bread.

5. By reason of the voice of my groaning my bones cleave to my skin.

Some days after Jackie's death, I was not hungry. Food did not want to go down. When I was alone, I did not eat, could not eat, and the grief was unbearable.

6. I am like a pelican of the wilderness: I am like an owl of the desert.

7. I watch and am as a sparrow alone upon the housetop.

I felt alone, like no one cared. There are days that I don't speak to anyone, no one comes by, and no one calls. I jokingly told one of my grandchildren if I died on Sunday afternoon at four, no one would know it until the following Sunday at noon.

8. Mine enemies reproach me all the day, and they that are mad against me are sworn against me.

9. For I have eaten ashes like bread; and mingled my drink with weeping.

10. Because of thine indignation and thy wrath: for thou has lifted me up and cast me down.

11. My days are like a shadow that declineth; and I am withered like grass.

Today, as I read this Psalm, the Lord spoke to me in a way that He has not in a long time. These words became my words, and these words of pain and suffering were what I was feeling inside. I was overwhelmed and broken, just as David was when he wrote these words. Thank you, God, for hearing my cry and answering my prayers.

12 But thou, O Lord, shall endure forever; and thy remembrance unto all generations.

13 Thou shalt arise, and have mercy upon Zion: for the time to favour her, yea, the set time, is come.

[14] For thy servants take pleasure in her stones and favour the dust thereof.

[15] So the heathen shall fear the name of the LORD, and all the kings of the earth thy glory.

[16] When the LORD shall build up Zion, he shall appear in his glory.

[17] He will regard the prayer of the destitute and not despise their prayer.

[18] This shall be written for the generation to come: and the people which shall be created shall praise the LORD.

[19] For he hath looked down from the height of his sanctuary; from heaven did the LORD behold the earth;

[20] To hear the groaning of the prisoner; to loose those that are appointed to death;

[21] To declare the name of the LORD in Zion, and his praise in Jerusalem;

[22] When the people are gathered together, and the kingdoms, to serve the LORD.

[23] He weakened my strength in the way; he shortened my days.

[24] I said, O my God, take me not away in the midst of my days: thy years are throughout all generations.

25 Of old hast thou laid the foundation of the earth: and the heavens are the work of thy hands.

26 They shall perish, but thou shalt endure: yea, all of them shall wax old like a garment; as a vesture shalt thou change them, and they shall be changed:

27 But thou art the same, and thy years shall have no end.

28 The children of thy servants shall continue, and their seed shall be established before thee.

103 Bless the LORD, O my soul: and all that is within me, bless his holy name.

2 Bless the LORD, O my soul, and forget not all his benefits:

3 Who forgiveth all thine iniquities; who healeth all thy diseases;

4 Who redeemeth thy life from destruction; who crowneth thee with lovingkindness and tender mercies;

5 Who satisfieth thy mouth with good things; so that thy youth is renewed like the eagle's.

Bless the Lord. He has forgiven me, healed me, redeemed me, and satisfied me. He has renewed me, just like an eagle. How is that? How is an eagle renewed?

An eagle goes through many stages from the time it is hatched until it is full-grown. It starts with soft white fuzz and changes as it grows through stages until it is the giant, majestic bird we know and recognize. There is nothing as heart-touching or as magnificent as a bald eagle in flight in all of its glory. We can soar like an eagle when we are in place, in touch where God wants us to be.

32

MY FIRST CHRISTMAS ALONE

IT'S MY FIRST Christmas without Jackie, but I was accustomed to shopping alone; he did not like to shop. He would sometimes go with me when I put him on a guilt trip, which I did once in a while.

On this day, I went to Wal-Mart to pick up a few things, getting a Christmas package ready to send to Kristopher, my grandson, who is now in the Marines. I found everything but one item, so I was stopping by Target. I had one goal as I pulled into the parking lot. I was there to get Kristopher's present and go home. I was tired, and my feet hurt, so I was in and on my way out in less than 20 min. What a relief!

I stood by the door at Target getting my keys out, so I wouldn't have to juggle the bags and search in my purse for the keys once I got outside. I finally put the bags down and emptied my purse. The keys were not there, nor were they in my pocket or anywhere else around me.

I walked back over my path about four times, asked the cashier, and they were not there. Fortunately, I ran into my friend, Diane, and she helped me look all over the store another three or four times. We walked outside again with no luck. We re-checked inside, and no keys anywhere. The cashier told us to check the car's inside to see if they fell in the side pocket – the doors are locked. Then leave your name and number, and we will call if someone turns them in - I have to stay here; I don't have another car or house key. We took one more trip back through the store, following my steps. Diane suggested we find the girl who checked us out; maybe she put the keys into her pocket and thought they were hers. We found her, and nope, she didn't have them. Would we like her to check by the register? I told her no; someone had already looked twice. However, Diane said, "Yes, please?"

Guess where my keys were? In a drawer where she had put them. Thank you, Diane! It only took two hours for me to do 15 minutes of shopping, but that's what Grandmas do! Kristopher will get his present, and that is all that matters. Thank you for serving in the US Marines, Kristopher. We love you & will miss you at Christmas, but you will be here in our hearts!

33

GOD CONTINUES TO BLESS AND PROVIDE

January 4, 2013, The days are sometimes challenging, but family and friends are helping. I have made it through our anniversary, his birthday, Thanksgiving, and Christmas, and I miss him so much.

I am still amazed as God continues to provide in ways I never imagined. A friend, Allison, and I traveled to Ireland and England. She and her husband are two of the kindest and most compassionate people I have ever met.

My group of friends (G.I.R.L.S.–Girls In Real-Life Situations) that I graduated with continue to get me for lunch or stop by to visit. God supplies all my needs and provides me with friends who love and care for me. Thank you, Patt, Charlynne, Jeanne, Sandy, Bubbles, Sue, Joanne, Pam, Linda, Elaine, Elisabeth, Glaconia, and Glenda. Patt and Charly have become close friends, and we get together or talk on the phone more often. They have made a tremendous difference in my life, and I am so thankful for them.

Our family continues to grow, and I now have a great-grand-daughter, Parker. Another great-grandson will soon join her in April and a great-granddaughter in May. New life, good times, and love of family help to make the bad times less. Jackie is forever in my thoughts, and each day my goal is to live "One Day At A Time."

(2020 - We now have more Great-Grandchildren, Trenton, Gracie, Parker, Easton, Haley, Chase, Zane, Zoey, and Olive.)

The last two weeks have been hard. I have cried at least half the day every day. The emptiness and loneliness fill your entire body, and all you can do is sob. I just want him to come home. I want him to talk to me and tell me what to do. Do I keep the Jeep, sell the Jag, sell both, and get a new one? How long can I work and pay this high rent? This house is too big, where do I move? What will I do for money when I can't work anymore? How do I get all of our family together again? It seems as if we grow further apart instead of closer together.

Wow, what has happened? I lost sight of my goal of living One Day At A Time and trusting God to supply all my needs. My faith is weak. My heart is broken, but I know God can heal. He told me so, and we had an excellent talk today. He will supply all our needs!

. . .

May 1, 2013

I can't believe it has been a year. The days seem long, and yet the weeks fly by. My family and friends have stood by me this past year, and I am thankful for all of them, but most of all, I am grateful to God for his tender mercies and grace. He has supplied my needs and answered prayer, and I know I am truly blessed.

I have a fantastic job with Datavision that I love and wonderful friends/family God has placed in my life, Sudharshan, Sherry, Neel, Jay, and Dev.

God is good, and as I remembered back a year ago, today it is with much pain and sorrow, but through it all, He has supplied the strength I need to go forward, One Day At A Time. There have been many bumps in the road, but this helps us to grow. Thank you all for your love and support.

. . .

May 16, 2013

Thank you all for the Birthday Wishes. I received the best gift tonight when Jason came out of surgery with his foot and all of his toes. I thank God for a miracle today. We did not get to talk to the doctor, so we do not know all that he did or how much he had to take out. Jason will still have a long way to go for this to get well, and he will be off work for a while, but God is good, and tonight, we are thanking Him for his compassion and love. Thank all of you for praying for us and for praying for the doctors. I thank God that when we left the hospital a little while ago, Jason was awake, hungry, and thirsty. Above all, we are thankful for our God, who hears and answers prayer. I am blessed beyond measure and I love all of you, my family, and my friends. I would ask that you keep our family in your prayers. (PS: Update 12/19/2016: Jason was off work for over a year, continues to have some issues with his foot because of Diabetes. He can work, and we know it is only the grace of God that allows him to do all that he does. Things could have been very different.) Update 10/30/20 Jason is now medically retired and still off his foot more than he can walk on it. He lost that little toe, eventually. God is still God!

Facebook, June 6, 2013: Time goes by so quickly. Sometimes we need to slow down and take the time to say what we want to say before our time is almost over, and we say, remember when.... It seems like yesterday that Isaac, Daphne, Jason, and James were small and underfoot...and now Isaac and Daphne have grandchildren. Where did the years go?

34

HAPPY ANNIVERSARY SWEETHEART

TODAY, JUNE 7, 2013, would have been our 50th anniversary. We were planning a big celebration for this day, but God had another celebration in mind for Jackie, and he had to leave me. We will catch up on our anniversary when I get there.

Happy Anniversary Sweetheart, June 7, 2014

It has been hard to find words to describe what I feel today. On May 1, it was two years since Jackie passed away. It seems like much longer. He was the light of my life, and I miss him as much today as I did when he left. I see couples today who fall in and out of love, like changing shoes. They have no idea what love is. It is not what you can do for each other; it is not what you offer each other in worldly treasures, but what you have to give from your heart - Love, Unconditional Love. I thought when we got married; I was supposed to be June Cleaver, keep a perfect house, and have dinner on the table when he came home from work. That all changed when the children come along, and it is hard to get the house cleaned, clothes washed (on a wringer washer), and dinner on the table. Forget about combing your hair and putting lipstick on. That's where the love is. It is doing it all together and facing a crisis together, in sickness and in health. I have never been and will never be a June Cleaver.

There were so many times in our life we could have said, let's just give up; it will never work. Too many bills, not enough time, and never enough money. The car broke down, the water heater broke, and the kids are sick.

The grass always looks greener --- from a distance. When you make it through all the rough stuff, you look back and say that made you stronger, and you plunge ahead to the next crisis. You do it together. That's love!

Love and marriage are hard work, meaning you have to be committed to making it work. Commitment and Dedication are two words most people do not think about concerning marriage. So, what is love? It is staying together when times are rough. It is holding each other's hands when your hearts are broken. It is holding each other close, so the two of you can stand together because there will be times you are so full of grief and pain you cannot stand alone. A case of united you stand! It is in knowing no matter what happens in your life; you will not be alone......................................until he is gone.

Love doesn't end when your heartbreaks, the pain never goes away, and the tears still come often. Life will never be the same.

What is love? Only your heart can tell you, and only you will know. Work at it, and then suddenly, one day, you see that you can never let him go and be a complete person again. I sat with Jackie almost every minute of the last nine months of his life. Despite that, I wonder if I could have or should have done anything differently.

Only God can heal a broken heart, and only God can give you the peace you need. I have a broken heart that God is healing, but even more, I have the peace of God in knowing I will see him again. It's been two years, and now I am two years closer to seeing him again.

35

REMEMBER THE LITTLE THINGS!

DEC 19, 2014 - This will be my third Christmas without Jackie, and sometimes I let it get overwhelming. I have shared with you many times we learned to live One Day at A Time as we went through his sickness. Facing today's problems today and knowing tomorrow, there may be more, but those problems we face tomorrow.

A lesson learned from Matthew 6:26-34.

I have heard the comment so often, "Life goes on," and yes, it does, but so does grief. It doesn't end after a year or two years or three. I am not sure it ever ends. That doesn't mean we roll around in our sorrow with a puppy dog face and look for sympathy. It does mean sometimes tears roll down your face, and you have no control over it. It happened to me when I went to get the tag for his car this year, and the ladies told me I needed to get it in my name. Just thinking about it as we talked made the tears roll, not only mine but theirs as well. I bit my lip, put my head down, and took a deep breath. I didn't want to cry, but I couldn't help it. It just seems like a little of him disappears every day, and I don't want to forget him.

Fortunately for me, the ladies knew me and could understand me as I sobbed. They apologized while passing the tissues, telling me I had to go back to the bank first to pick up the title. I felt terrible as I sobbed, but I couldn't help it. When I arrived at the bank where they all knew him, they started crying as soon as they saw me with papers in my hand. Finally, I made it back to DMV, and they changed the title and gave me my sticker.

Tears start when I am sitting in church, and I see a couple, and his arm is around her. I want to tell them to appreciate it now because it hurts later when you are sitting alone. Things we take for granted! It's the little things in life that you will miss the most. For those of you who know me well, it is missing him at home in the morning with my coffee ready, cooking, cleaning, and spoiling me rotten. I find two or three pairs of shoes by the door now and realize I have to move them now without being reminded that I will break my neck tripping over them. Little things!

Grief also means there are many nights; you cry yourself to sleep. Just this week, the song that kept going through my mind when I went to bed one night was, "I cry myself to sleep each night, wishing I could hold you tight." Then I realized that if I thought of another song like "Thank you, Lord, for your blessings on me," it makes a lot of difference in the way you feel. I may not have everything I want, but it is also true, I have much more than I need. God has blessed me tremendously, and I am thankful. Christmas is not a time to be sad because it was always a happy family time, which needs to continue. Christmas is different, but Jesus is still the reason for the season! Family time and traditions continue. On Saturday, my grandson Kristopher and Kate will get married, so we add one more to the family. Many things have changed over the years, but one thing remains the same: Family! When we get together on Christmas Eve, it will still be different, but we will think of Jackie, Papa Jack with love. Gone, but not forgotten.

Remember this Christmas season; some family members will not be here next year or even tomorrow. Live today for today and spend today as if it were your last day. What would you tell your family and friends if you knew it was the last time you would see them?

Just some thoughts today for you!

. . .

May 1, 2015 Today is three years since Jackie passed away, but I will always have memories of our years together. He loved me unconditionally, and most people will never have a love like this in the world today. I am so thankful that God allowed us the time we had together, but it makes each day even harder to face without him. Today, May 1, is just one more reminder that he is gone. However, one thing that stays with me is the memories I have hidden in my heart.

There can never be another love like this for me, and as I watch couples in different places, I see the interaction between them. In the church, I will see a couple and his arm is on the back of the pew behind her, and I can't help but remember all the times his arm was not behind me but across my shoulders or if his back was hurting, and he couldn't sit a certain way he would hold my hand, always a physical touch. I want to tell these couples that life is short and never take each other for granted.

I see the smiling faces in restaurants as families eat together, and I want to tell all of them to enjoy this today and tuck it in your heart because one day, these memories will be all you have. You will remember every silly argument since no marriage is perfect, and no human is perfect. There will always be differences. Just remember, one day, you will look back and think why in the world did it matter, so choose your battles wisely.

Today is a date that brought sorrow, and yes, facing today will be a challenge, but life goes on. Since he left, many things have changed, and Jackie would be proud of all his family. We love him and miss him today and every day.

36

I WILL NEVER FORGET WHEN YOUR HEART STOPPED AND MINE KEPT BEATING!

IT HAS BEEN four years tomorrow, May 1, 2016, since Jackie passed away, and it seems like an eternity ago. I think about him every day and this week, even more than usual. It is not always sad but sometimes, like today, when he would have laughed at me and reminded me why he always called me Dollbaby. (Dolls have a stuffed body and empty head.)

I went outside intending to water the plants, so I pulled the hose off the roller. Then I noticed the sprinkler was attached rather than a nozzle, so I tried to take it off but couldn't turn it. I went back into the house for my "work" gloves, came back, and twisted until my fingers were in the shape of a figure 8 before it loosened up. Man, that was tough; then, I noticed something still attached to the end of the hose, and it would not come off sprinkler guts! Guess it will never work again.

No problem, there's another hose with the hoe sitting on it, although it looks pretty old and could be dry rotted. I moved the hoe from where it was sitting and hung it in the rack. Then I immediately turned around, pulling the hose, which knocked the hoe off, and it hit me on the head. There was no problem, hardhead, and no damage, not even a scratch.

While I am right here with the rake, shovel, hoe, and there is a pile of leaves under the pump house, I knew I should rake them back out of the way, so I did..done! Now, on to the old rotten hose. I put the nozzle on it, pulled it over to the first plant, got a kink in the hose, so I lay it down, letting the water run while I get the kink out! I pulled the hose, knocked the little fence thing over on the plant, and broke it.

Moving along to the front yard, I see the "Zombie" cat as Zoey has named it—neighbor's cat - he is lying in the dry birdbath. Guess I should put some water in it now while I have the hose up here. I cleaned it out and filled it with water. Then I watered all the plants in the flower beds that Sam and I had redone with mulch and potting soil.

Here is another lesson I learned. If you're alone and can't pick up the gigantic bag of potting soil in your trunk, just back your car up, flip the bag over and out. Then you can leave it leaning on the car while you carry all the pots from the backyard and fill them up, then carry them all back, one or two at a time.

While I have the hose out here, I need to wash all the pollen off the porch since I seem to have some allergies and can't talk 3/4ths of the time. There are some flying critters with a nest, and it is trying to keep predators away by stinging them. I hope it is like a bee and dies after stinging because it sure hurts. It stung me on top of a burn I got from trying to get a piece of Trenton's pizza crust out of the bottom of the oven last night.

After watering the plants on the back porch and backyard, I notice an enormous pile of small trees, vines, and palmetto plants all piled up that I cut down a couple of days ago. I thought about burning them, but I am not doing anything I don't have to do with my luck the last few days. Besides, I don't want to burn the house down.

So, I miss Jackie today and every day. There is hardly a day that goes by when I don't cry. He was the love of my life, and I was his. Despite all the dumb crazy things I did and still do, he thought I was perfect and loved me anyway. If he were here today, he would have said, "Dollbaby, you go inside. I'll finish this." Then he would have laughed and finished it all in about 5 minutes. It's the little things that mean so much. Not the diamonds, gold, or a Jaguar! It was holding my hand, making me laugh, and loving me no matter what the situation.

There are many times that grief will come unexpectedly, just like waves on the ocean begin with a slight ripple if, given the right weather, those ripples will turn into gigantic waves. Maybe you're driving alone in your car, washing the dishes, or watching TV when suddenly a tsunami hits. Feeling all the grief makes you realize how so very MUCH you miss him. As you try to catch your breath, your tears flow, and the sadness is so great it is physically painful.

All I wanted to do today was water the flowers, which I did, but I cried, and I laughed and thought of the half of my heart that is in Heaven! I miss you so much today, tomorrow, forever!

37

WHAT IS LOVE?

February 14, 2019–For You On Valentine's Day!

Valentine's Day is supposed to be one of the most romantic days of the year. How can we celebrate this day to make it memorable and unique for the one we love? We want it to be a special day they will never forget.

Here is what I have learned: Treat the person you love this same way every day. It's not the day, the card, or a present; it's the fact that you want to show them your love. Every day with your loved one should be treated as a remarkable one and leave an impression–not just Valentine's Day! The thing is, sometimes we don't realize how much we love them until they are gone, so let me tell you this story.

It has been really hard to find words to describe what I feel today. On Feb. 14, 2019, it will be six years, nine months, and 13 days since Jackie passed away. He was the light of my life, and I miss him as much today as I did when he left.

Love doesn't end when your heart breaks; the pain never goes away, and the tears still come often. Life will never be the same. I have heard that that time heals all wounds. My grief has lessened some, but I don't believe it will ever go away, and my scar tissue has not fully covered enough to keep the pain out. Grief never ends, but it is not a place to stay; it is not a sign of weakness or even a lack of faith. Grief is a price we pay for genuine love.

What is love? Only your heart can tell you, and only you will know. You must continually work at it, and then suddenly, one day, you know you can never let him go and be a complete person again.

I sat with Jackie almost every minute of the last nine months of his life, and yet, I wonder if I could have or should have done anything differently. I look back at his pictures now, and I can see how cancer gradually took him away from me. He tried so hard to get well because he knew that is what we wanted. Finally, he just got so tired he couldn't do it anymore. With the last of his strength, his hand touched my arm, and our eyes met. He looked into my eyes, and with his last breath, whispered, "Please." I knew he was asking me to let him go, and I loved him so much, I had to say, "OK." Then he peacefully closed his eyes and was home.

Could I have spoken differently during those months when he was weak and ill? Could I have shown more compassion? The list could go on and on, but it doesn't matter now; it's too late to do things differently!

A few months after Jackie died, I visited Ireland and England with our friend Allison. When we visited Buckingham Palace, there were so many amazing things to see. Beautiful Diamond Crowns and jewelry were on display, and yes, I drooled all over the place, being the diamond lover I am. They were impressive, but what got my attention was not the diamonds, the shining chandeliers, or beautiful statues and art, but the inscription on the glass enclosure covering one of Queen Victoria's gowns. If you know history, you know her husband and father of their nine children died after 21 years of marriage. The inscription tells you what real heartfelt love and grief are. "My life as a happy one is ended! The world is gone for me!" She never recovered from his death and mourned the rest of her life.

Do I still miss Jackie after all these years? Yes, I think about him every day. Our special days are even harder, but I don't want to live like my world is gone. We have a fantastic family and incredible friends. Yes, some days are harder than others, but there are more happy days than sad ones. God is healing my broken heart, but more importantly, He assures me and gives me the peace of knowing that I will see Jackie again.

Please remember this: Today could be your last day with those you love. Show them every day how much you love them; telling them isn't enough. **It is how you live that shows your love.** It can be a smile, a touch, or the words you speak.

Love lives and breathes: you can see it.

Begin today, showing your love and sharing the meaning of what true love means while you still have the opportunity because you will always question yourself no matter how much you say and do...... so do the most you can!

If you ask me today If I knew how much he loved me, My answer to the question would be, "Yes." His day on Earth ended on May 1, 2012. His tomorrow did not come, and I knew how much he loved me. If you knew him, you knew the answer too. It was a love you could see, and I know now how blessed we were to share that love for almost 49 years.

As I look back today, I see him in his life as a fighter. Even when cancer had weakened his body, a severed artery had paralyzed his vocal cord, and he could no longer walk, talk, eat, or swallow. I see him as an example to our children, grandchildren, and great-grandchildren.

I look around our house, and today, the place is different; the furniture and décor are the same. I see things we bought together and shared, but even more importantly, I see pictures of a family that he always put first, no matter what else was happening. It could be a phone call to ask Papa Jack a question, directions, or a visit to ask for advice, or just to talk; he was always there.

Our worldly possessions are not the most important things as we live and look back on our lives, but the greatest possession we can have is the precious memories created by taking the time and never being too busy for our family. If tomorrow never comes, will they know how much you love them? Without a doubt, I can tell you our children, grandchildren & one of our nine great-grandchildren all know how much he loved them. I can also guarantee you they still feel his hugs, even after all these years. I know because I can. Love is the greatest gift one generation can leave to another. Make sure you do that today because one day, your tomorrow will not come.

I will only add one thing to all of this: As we live each day expectantly, take a deep breath, and focus on trusting God, living One Day At A Time! He can and will supply all your needs in His Time, Every Time!

Our four children, Isaac, Jason, Daphne, and James.

Isaac & Cheryl, Ian & Taylor, Jenny & Ricky –
Zoey–Olive

Daphne & T.J., Samuel,
Joshua & Kristin– Haley–Chase–Zane
Jesse & Melody–Trenton–Gracie–Parker–Easton

Jason & Tina, Kristopher & Kate, Cassie & Mae

James & Julie - Gentry

Thank you for your love and support every day! I Love You!

A SPECIAL THANK YOU!

I went to work with Datavision Technologies, a fantastic company, a few months after Jackie passed away. To Sherry Marek and Sudharshan Chary, two amazing people in my life who comforted, supported, and brought joy back into my life when I needed it most, thank you. I am profoundly thankful and blessed to have been a part of this company. I had the opportunity to travel to different cities in the US, Spain, and Holland. I met many wonderful people in the Hospitality World at HFTP/HITEC, HUG, and various conferences, thanks to this position with Datavision. I retired on June 30, 2020 and would like to thank all the Hospitality World for the opportunity to have spent time with you.